Reviews from the first edition

This is the book I have been waiting for. Ever since I first started working with teachers on preservice and inservice programs (US) and teacher training and inset courses (UK) in the 1980s, I wished there were a book that presented seminal studies in education and psychology in an accessible way, and drawing out implications for practice. This is it. In this wonderfully readable book, Bradley Busch and Edward Watson present 77 key studies from education and psychology, spanning over 60 years that every teacher should know about. Whether you are just beginning as a teacher, or a seasoned veteran, there will be something here that will be directly relevant to your practice and, perhaps more importantly, will make you think. Highly recommended.

Dylan Wiliam, Emeritus Professor of Educational Assessment, University College London, UK

This book will prove irresistible to anyone keen to understand more about essential educational research findings in the most accessible manner possible. The authors identify the most influential and important findings of research relating to key issues in classrooms such as effective teaching, student behaviours, the impact of family and practice that develops skilled learners. Busch and Watson offer a concise, punchy and engaging resource for everyone seeking to help children and young people learn in the most effective way. An absolute must for every school.

Professor Dame Alison Peacock, Chief Executive, The Chartered College of Teaching, UK

The Science of Learning is a timely and precious gift to teachers. We know that research and evidence, used well, are vital complements to teachers' experience and professional judgement, but finding the most relevant research, understanding what it shows, and knowing how to implement these findings accurately can be really tricky. No wonder that, despite the burgeoning interest in research among teachers, there is still limited application of research in teachers' practice. This book provides an appealing and trustworthy solution: a range of fascinating studies – from large-scale and replicated to small and quirky – has been selected and their findings summarised with brilliant clarity. The discussions are brief but nuanced, and the sections on "classroom implications" offer thoughtful suggestions about how this knowledge can inform teachers' practice. The explanations are simple but not simplistic – a remarkable achievement. Interpreting research accurately and applying it intelligently are not easy tasks. This book has made them far easier. Every teacher should be given a copy.

Jonnie Noakes, Head of Teaching and Learning, Eton College, UK

This is the educational research book I have been waiting for!

As a profession, it is important that we are evidence-informed so that our most precious resource – time – is well spent on activities that will have the most impact on learning and progress for our students. But we are caught in the Catch-22 scenario of not having enough time to engage fully with the research studies themselves. Add to this the problems of academic paywalls, complex and frequently impenetrable presentation and language style, and the sheer volume of educational research available, and the opportunity cost becomes too high for a busy teacher to read the journal articles that might just help them be more effective.

Fortunately, Busch and Watson have the solution in this instantly accessible summary of 77 vital research studies that every teacher should know. The vibrant, infographic-style presentation leaps off the page, and the structure of the book lends itself to browsing and dipping in-and-out rather than cover-to-cover reading. You can digest the key findings from an important study in just a few minutes – ideal for a busy teacher, whether in training, in the first few years of their career or wearing the badge of experience.

The studies themselves are well-chosen, covering the fields of memory, motivation and metacognition as well as behaviour, bias and parenting. The interleaved structure encourages the reader to see the connections between the studies too, building up a coherent overall picture of what might actually work in the classroom.

Busch and Watson have come up with that rarity: an educational must-read. I will be recommending it to every teacher I know!

Chris Hildrew, Headteacher, Churchill Academy, UK

Two key questions facing classroom teachers today are: firstly, what research do I need to know? and secondly, how can I use it in my classroom? This book is a highly practicable guide to the often-impenetrable field of education research and is a very useful compass for school leaders, classroom teachers and parents alike in seeking which evidence-based strategies to implement.

Carl Hendrick, Author, *What Does This Look Like in the Classroom?*, UK

Like me, I trust you will enjoy reading, dipping into, thinking about, following up, questioning and asking for more – as you touch this book. This is my "book of the decade".

John Hattie, Laureate Professor, Melbourne University, Australia

The presentation of the topics in 77 succinct sections make this a really accessible, easy to use book. It's not daunting to just tackle one topic at a time, and in total the articles add up to really practical and useful knowledge, presented clearly.

Sarah Brew, *Parents in Touch*

If you're a teacher who wants to find out about many interesting findings from educational research, without having to spend precious free periods or leisure time looking for it, you should buy this book. And if you're a team leader, buying a copy for each member of your team would not be a bad investment – especially if you used selected studies as the basis for team discussions.

Terry Freedman, *Schools Week*

This is a really excellent resource for the busy teacher, education student or study support tutor with plenty of food for thought and easy to understand classroom or teaching suggestions.

Jan Beechey MCILIP, *Dyslexia Review*

THE SCIENCE OF LEARNING

Supporting teachers in the quest to help students learn as effectively and efficiently as possible, *The Science of Learning* translates 99 of the most important and influential studies on the topic of learning into accessible and easily digestible overviews. Building on the bestselling original book, this second edition delves deeper into the world of research into what helps students learn, with 22 new studies covering key issues including cognitive-load theory, well-being and performing well under exam pressure.

Demystifying key concepts and translating research into practical advice for the classroom, this unique resource will increase teachers' understanding of crucial psychological research so they can help students improve how they think, feel and behave in school. From large- to small-scale studies, from the quirky to the iconic, the book breaks down complicated research to provide teachers with the need-to-know facts and implications of each study. Each overview combines graphics and text, asks key questions, describes related research and considers implications for practice. Highly accessible, each overview is attributed to one of seven key categories:

- Memory: increasing how much students remember
- Mindset, motivation and resilience: improving persistence, effort and attitude
- Self-regulation and metacognition: helping students to think clearly and consistently
- Student behaviours: encouraging positive student habits and processes
- Teacher attitudes, expectations and behaviours: adopting positive classroom practices
- Parents: how parents' choices and behaviours impact their children's learning
- Thinking biases: avoiding faulty thinking habits that get in the way of learning

A hugely accessible resource, this unique book will support, inspire and inform teaching staff, parents and students, and those involved in leadership and CPD.

Edward Watson is the founder of InnerDrive, UK.

Bradley Busch is a chartered psychologist at InnerDrive, UK.

THE SCIENCE OF LEARNING

99 Studies That Every Teacher Needs to Know

Second Edition

Edward Watson and Bradley Busch

Routledge
Taylor & Francis Group

LONDON AND NEW YORK

Second edition published 2021
by Routledge
2 Park Square, Milton Park, Abingdon, Oxon, OX14 4RN

and by Routledge
52 Vanderbilt Avenue, New York, NY 10017

Routledge is an imprint of the Taylor & Francis Group, an informa business

First edition published by Routledge 2019

British Library Cataloguing-in-Publication Data
A catalogue record for this book is available from the British Library

Library of Congress Cataloging-in-Publication Data
Names: Watson, Edward, author. | Busch, Bradley, author.
Title: The science of learning: 99 studies that every teacher needs to know/Edward Watson and Bradley Busch.
Description: 2nd edition. | Abingdon, Oxon; New York, NY: Routledge, 2021. | Includes bibliographical references.
Identifiers: LCCN 2020047352 | ISBN 9780367620844 (hardback) | ISBN 9780367620790 (paperback) | ISBN 9781003107866 (ebook)
Subjects: LCSH: Learning, Psychology of. | Learning - Research. | Teaching-Research.
Classification: LCC LB1060 .B875 2021 | DDC 370.15/23–dc23
LC record available at https://lccn.loc.gov/2020047352

ISBN: 978-0-367-62084-4 (hbk)
ISBN: 978-0-367-62079-0 (pbk)
ISBN: 978-1-003-10786-6 (ebk)

Typeset in Interstate
by Apex CoVantage, LLC

BB: To Pippa, thank you for teaching me so much. To my not-so-little-big-boy Jacob, I hope you keep learning it all.

ETW: To Helen, Izzy, Ollie, Twiggy and Pavlov; thanks for putting up with my failings, for celebrating my successes and for being with me during the journey between the two.

From both of us, a big thank you to Routledge, our publishers, for taking a chance on us. A special thanks to Clare, whose original idea paved the way for this book and to both Annamarie and Alice, whose help, support and patience has been invaluable.

To our wonderfully talented graphics designer, Luis, a big thank you! We love your beautiful artwork – your creative talents are essential and much appreciated.

Thank you to the many researchers whose studies we have described. We hope that we have done your research the justice it deserves. And finally, thank you to all the members (past and present) of the InnerDrive team. In particular, thanks to DC, Blythe, Marayka, Emily, Izzy, Tom, Grace, Hattie, Ruhee, George, Ludmilla and Matt. We have loved working with you all. A big thank you also to Dan – we couldn't have done any of this without you.

CONTENTS

TIPS   205

ABOUT THE AUTHORS

Edward Watson is a graduate of Oxford University who served seven years in the Army. After receiving an MBA at The London Business School, he worked as a strategic management consultant for Marakon Associates before running businesses in the computer games market. As well as working in the corporate, education and sport sectors, he is also the co-author of *Release Your Inner Drive*.

Bradley Busch is a chartered psychologist. With extensive experience working in schools, he is a leading expert at helping schools utilise psychological research. Outside of education, Bradley works with elite athletes that include England international footballers and members of Team GB. He is the co-author of *Release Your Inner Drive*.

If you want to chat to Edward or Bradley about The Science of Learning, *or about staff and student workshops, you can email them on info@innerdrive.co.uk.*

FOREWORD FROM THE FIRST EDITION

In the good ol' days, research went through a peer-review process, was published, subject to replication and falsification, and followed rules of behaviour that have been handed down and refined since the 16th century. The basic premise was to follow Newton's dictum to stand on the shoulders of giants and continually add, refine and interpret the evidence in these published articles. But there was a late-20th-century explosion in the volume of evidence, an opening (via the internet) to access this volume of research, and the older rules of who published and what was published were questioned and often discarded. We are now in the days of evidence – mountains of it. The calls to use evidence are now everywhere, from politicians, parent groups, policy makers and educators – but whose evidence?

At the same time, the growth of denialism has exploded, and we have major world leaders using denial as the basis of popularist electioneering: fake news, "lies, damn lies, and statistics", skills in clickbaiting, never letting evidence get in the way of a good argument (especially when it is my argument). We are indeed in the days of "post-truth" (the OED word of the year for 2016). "Truth is dead, facts are passé". Rhetorical effluent, passing the pub test, the smell test are the new norms.

My own exploration of this phenomena began when I noted that every educator seemed to know the secret to making schools successful – and the answer seemed to be what they were researching. And they had evidence, buckets of it, to support their claim. I was a student in these schools once and many of these claims did not ring true. My venture was to change the debate from "what works" to "what works best" and to ask the relativity question. Then, the pursuit of evidence – in my case, the synthesis of meta-analyses to create a relative ordering of effective interventions. Perhaps the most surprising news was that more than 95% of the interventions we implement to enhance student achievement work! I then wanted to change the bar – asking not what improves achievement but what discriminates between those interventions with high compared to lower positive effects. Ninety thousand studies, one-quarter of a billion students and 250 influences later, there is a set of claims – and, not surprisingly, my interpretations are hotly contested (as they should be).

Perhaps the days of asking for more evidence are passing. Given the volume of "evidence", maybe it is time to move past asking for more evidence and ask for more interpretation and dissemination of the evidence. The Education Endowment Fund is an exemplar at this translation, but more is needed. Perhaps an even greater need is to have more effective models for implementing the translation of evidence. I very much like the notion of "translation", as it puts the emphasis on those translating to ensure that the reader actually understands - otherwise there is no or poor translation. This is possibly the next most exciting development in our research world - translating the research so that it can be more readily implemented.

Here is where this book makes a major advance. When the authors sent me the page on my work to fact-check, I was seriously impressed with their skills of taking big ideas and presenting them in digestible form - without talking down, without missing key moderators and with much panache. The combination of the visual and verbal is impressive, the 77 major messages of high importance and the layout easy to navigate.

Take two of their messages: studying words and pictures together led to correctly answering more than twice as many questions as those who had revised with only words or with only pictures; and "the one about picturing the process". They obviously listened to themselves, as the book is structured around the research on these two messages. Not only are the pictures perfect for ease of understanding, for use in professional development and for implications for practice, but they also provide the original references and hot tips at the end.

In 1921, Fred Barnard devised an ad using the phrase: "one look is worth a thousand words" and claimed it was "a Chinese proverb so people would take it seriously". Bradley Busch and Edward Watson have certainly taken the research on cognitive and neuroscience seriously and turned thousands of words into magnificent pictures. And this is the skill that leads to more effective implementation of research that is so sorely needed in these days of evidence.

Like me, I trust you will enjoy reading, dipping into, thinking about, following up, questioning and asking for more - as you touch this book. This is my "book of the decade" and may there be many more like this.

John Hattie

HOW TEACHERS USE IT

Our aim is for this book to inform and stimulate discussion about the science of learning and its application to classroom teaching. Here are some ideas about how to use the book more widely within teacher CPD from those who read the first edition:

> I've found the book *The Science of Learning* both interesting and helpful. Reading the classroom implications has been particularly useful, providing me with handy tips and methods to incorporate in my teaching. For example, I have applied the findings from Study 15 to my maths planning for Fractions, Decimals and Percentages. I spaced out the teaching of the material and in the lead up to the tests, ensured that there was a range of problems for the children to solve that required them to consider which skills they would need to employ. This approach meant that children felt more confident about the prospect of taking the tests and, for the most part, were pleased with the results.
>
> Study 42 was useful and had a positive impact on children's learning in maths. For example, knowing that they were about to be placed into random groups in maths for a mixed number/ improper fraction treasure hunt, increased their focus during the whole class explanation. They were told that all members of the group would be asked at the end of the activity to complete one question correctly before being declared the winners. Therefore, they realised the importance of being able to teach those who might experience difficulties with the concept. Another reason for increased focus was fear of letting the other group members down.
>
> We do the "Daily Mile" at our school, but Study 50 reminded me of the benefits of taking a break from learning and going for a walk. This is something that we do from time to time with positive results in terms of renewed energy and application.
>
> — Elaine Prendiville, Winnersh Primary School

Over the past year in my role as Assistant Principal i/c I have implemented a vision of research-based practice for all our CPD. This means that we think carefully as an SLT about what CPD we plan and make sure it is something which will have real proven impact in the classroom and is not a gimmick. We also always make sure that when we introduce any new strategies, that we communicate why we are introducing them and the benefit the change will have on pupils. For this reason, *The Science of Learning* has been crucial for us.

One key strategy we have implemented this year for example, is that of retrieval practice. Through delivering regular Teacher Learning Communities (small cross-subject groups) we outlined what retrieval practice is and some key ways it can be implemented for different subjects. However, the most important part of this process, was sharing what the evidence says. Through using the brilliant visual information in the book, we were able to communicate the Roediger and Karpicke study which outlined the testing effect and the benefits of retrieval over re-reading. We have seen over the past few months a huge increase in staff embedding retrieval practice into lessons and in turn more confidence and increasing amounts of knowledge by pupils. For example, the History department has implemented the pomodoro technique of revision using 20 minute blocks where pupils write down everything they remember about a topic and then only when they have exhausted this do they use a textbook to add in the extra information.

Most subjects are now starting lessons with a quiz or brain dump. "Flashback Friday" and "Throwback Thursday" are proving very popular! This is something we will continue to embed over the next few months and believe it is having a real effect on pupil progress. This is one example of how we have used the studies in the book, but it really is an invaluable resource for us both for classroom teachers and for SLT planning CPD.

- Rachel Ball, Co-op Academy, Walkden

The Science of Learning is incredibly important at my school as we have four key priorities with teaching and learning which are literacy, questioning, feedback and cognitive science. This is across the whole school and at a departmental level. The two areas my History department have been focusing on with regards to the science of learning are retrieval practice and dual coding. The sections in the book dedicated to memory have been very insightful, informative and helpful with our curriculum and lesson planning. It is a key aspect of our development plan and professional development. We have taken the research findings and discussed what the implications for these are in our day to day planning and practice. The science of learning has helped me to reflect on my lessons and adapt them to become more evidence informed.

As a result of reading the book, changes have been made with how we support students with their revision strategies both from an academic and pastoral perspective. I have also reflected on how and when I use retrieval strategies in the classroom. The main way I have adapted my teaching has been my focus on revision strategies and metacognition. The book has had the greatest impact on me in my pastoral role as a GCSE class form tutor. I regularly share the research from this book with my tutees to help them understand how they can apply it to their studies. Using information in this book I also created a presentation that I delivered to parents of students in Years 10 & 11 about how they can support their child with their studies, advising what their children should and should not do. Parents found this very useful and I think many parents would find the book very helpful too.

The research study that myself, my colleagues and students found the most surprising was about the impact of the presence of a mobile phone and how distracting it can be. This is really important and screen time is something that continues to be an issue. I also found the studies about listening to music when trying to study too.

Finally, the layout of this book is incredible. Trying to read academic research papers can be very problematic. They can be difficult to access, very lengthy and filled with academic jargon. This book does a great job at summarising key studies, some I was familiar with but many I wasn't. I think a misconception about this book is that people assume it is just about cognitive psychology and memory, but it goes far beyond. It covers a wide range of topics useful for any teacher, middle or senior leader as well as being accessible for students and parents too.
- Kate Jones, The British School Al Khubairat, Abu Dhabi

We at Loughborough Amherst School have been using *The Science of Learning* ever since I attended one of your courses. The book mirrors the course: really simple to follow and easy to just pick up quickly & then put down again in the middle of busy teaching lives. I love the fact that although the basic T&L concepts aren't necessarily new, they are explained really clearly so that everyone (pupils and parents as well) can understand the theory. The use of science to back up every point leaves no room for argument which pupils dispute why they absolutely can multitask and listen to music, talk and play on their phones all whilst also working! We have given every member of our staff a copy of the book - and it was worth every penny in terms of CPD that everyone can find something useful and inspirational from. Thank you to all at InnerDrive for your hard work and I can't wait to see the next book!
- Grace Davies, Loughborough Academy

Over the past year my role as a teacher of History has changed drastically. Personally, I am able to look at studies from researcher Khattab about student aspirations and expectations and realise that I need to encourage a lift in both of these in order for my students to progress. As a department, the structure of our curriculum and practice has been dictated by research rather than what is considered 'fashionable' at the time. This refreshing look at teaching has been informed and inspired by studies provided in *The Science of Learning*, ensuring that teachers are developing themselves through rigorous CPD sessions that are tailored for our needs.

As a CPD lead in the school, I have been able to refer back to the book to create resources for CPD sessions and foster meaningful conversations and discussions between the teachers in the school. One fundamental strategy to further the progress of pupils in the school that has been introduced this year is the use of retrieval practice. This has now been rolled out across the school, and staff are becoming more and more confident every time they use a certain retrieval method. Through using the visual accessibility of the book, we have been able to communicate the studies from Roediger and Karpicke around the benefits of re-reading for retrieval, as well as the Dunlosky study on improving long-term memory. This is just one example of how this book has aided our progress as a school. The positivity with which this has been received by members of staff within CPD groups has been incredibly encouraging and shows that using this book works.

– Brad Williams, Co-op Academy, Walkden

I've used *The Science of Learning* extensively when leading on Teaching and Learning at West Coventry Academy. I produced readers of key studies for teachers and based a lot of the whole-school CPD sessions I designed around the accessible, easily digestible infographics and summaries. Fellow educators who I introduced to the book never fail to be impressed by its clear and concise structure and the power of the research findings behind it.

– Bertram Richter, Coventry Academy

What I love most about this book is its versatility. I sat down to read this book for my own interest as a teacher but quickly realised how I could use it as a form tutor, a head of department and as a teacher. For example, we have read and discussed studies in form time before – I asked students to consider the article about sleeping patterns before they kept a 'sleep diary' to monitor their behaviour for 2 weeks and reflect on how their behaviour compared to that advocated in the study of your book.

I have been able to use the book is so many different ways because it is so readable. The layout and language means that it is accessible to all – and also enjoyable to read. There are so many education books out there that 'drag on' – they are a book when they could have been a blog post. The book by InnerDrive thus stands out – each page is valuable and insightful and there are no wasted words!

My teaching has changed because of the insights gained in the studies of the book. Again, another unique feature of the book is the ease with which you can dip into it – using the contents page to find a study and read it before tweaking your teaching behaviour the next day. This allows it to be a highly useful book that really does change your practice.

– Kate Stockings, Hamsptead School

Introducing the book with questions and challenges definitely worked with quizzical, cynical and conservative colleagues as it started interrogation and discussions. These have been raised in monthly videos produced by teachers and then shown and shared across the group. Each video has taken one study and discussed it in the context of schools with students from over eighty different learning backgrounds.

'The plan' had envisaged setting up discussion groups between teachers but we did not need to facilitate these – they occurred naturally. Some were amongst subject specialists, others with pastoral practitioners, some within schools, some across sites. Something that surprised me was how many non-teaching colleagues were suddenly demanding a copy, 'I work in a school – I want to know more about learning – so I can help the students more' was a sentiment I heard from sales colleagues, cleaners, activity co-ordinators and many other members of our teams. Once again, getting colleagues to ask questions was key.

- How can I help develop learning in my role (whatever it is)?
- How in my interactions with students can I get them talking about good practice in learning?
- Which myth do I want to bust this week?

Different schools across the group have used the book differently but these have included: line managers using it as a focus for observation feedback conversations, asking teachers to identify something they would like to develop; students presenting studies to each other in tutor time; boarding staff asking students which of the studies they have seen evidence of in their lessons, and each week one study is highlighted with posters around the schools.

No resource is perfect for all contexts, but the well-thumbed and annotated copies of this book lying around our schools is evidence that, in our context, giving every teacher a copy has been beneficial. As educators, sometimes we all need reminding that as well as being pastoral agents we are crafts people. We use the skills of our profession to fashion learning. This book gets us thinking about how to hone the skills and ensure that they what we do is based on research. Use it – don't just read it.

– George Casley, CATS College London

Introduction

What is the science of learning? It is the quest to help our students learn more effectively and efficiently. Despite there being a wealth of research on the science of learning, to date, much of it has failed to get into the hands of the people who need it the most - that is, teachers.

There are three probable reasons for this:

1   Most people aren't too sure where to look for this sort of research.
2   If you did know where to look, you either have to pay lots of money to read the journals or have a current university subscription.
3   If you do have access to these studies, some of them are very hard to read and make sense of. For instance, this is how one of the results from a study we really like appears in its journal:

$$\text{Rating}(k) = \beta_1 \, \text{rating}^{(k-1)} + \sum_{i(k-1)}^{i(k)} \beta_2 \, \text{shocks}^{(k)} + \beta_3 \, \text{variable term}^{(k)}$$

This book seeks to fix those problems.

Where we were

The first edition of *The Science of Learning* was born out of frustration that there was a wealth of research out there that was stuck behind paywalls, difficult to locate and not obviously translatable into practical strategies. And yet, as a profession, education was becoming more and more informed by the research, with the desire to understand what works best in different situations growing significantly.

Our aim was to assist and encourage that movement by providing a brief synopsis of studies that we found interesting and useful, along with a summary of some of the related research and key classroom implications. Above all, we wanted to make research findings accessible, the complex simple and the theoretical practical.

Where we are

So, did *The Science of Learning* achieve its goals? The book has been read by teachers in thousands of schools. We've had reports of teachers reading it in all corners of the world, including England, India, Australia and America. It is also currently being translated into Chinese, Korean and Spanish.

Why a second edition, then? The science of learning never stands still. Our understanding of the factors that help students learn best is constantly evolving and developing. With fascinating new research being produced on a daily basis, there simply were more studies that we wanted to include.

This book includes studies from researchers in England, America, China, New Zealand, Canada, Japan, Australia, Germany, Spain, France, Holland, Belgium and Israel. We hope you find them as interesting, helpful and thought-provoking as we did. Some of the studies we have chosen are iconic. Some are quirky. Some are large-scale and some have a small sample size. This second edition contains some that are very old, and many that are very recent. Some have tracked students for more than 40 years, whereas others were done in just one day. But what they all have in common is they help us to paint a picture of the science of learning.

Where we want to be

We started the first edition with a quote from the Scottish poet Andrew Lange, who once said that "some individuals use statistics as a drunk man uses lamp-posts – for support rather than for illumination". We think the same can be true for psychology research papers. Our understanding of how people learn is constantly developing – with new studies being released and some old studies failing to replicate. What we 'know' is not a fixed or static thing. Therefore, this book represents our current understanding based on psychological research.

We want this new edition to be used as a springboard for high-quality discussions in the staff room, which will drive real change in the classroom. Author, anthropologist and filmmaker Zora Neale Hurston once said that "research is formalised curiosity. It's poking and prying with a purpose". If this new edition of *The Science of Learning* is used as a foundation to spark debate, discussion and even disagreement, then we will be very happy.

We know that nothing works everywhere or all of the time. But using research as a platform to discuss why we do what we do and what we think best serves our students is a healthy place for education to be. If we all have that debate, all our students will benefit.

How We Wrote This Book

This book isn't written like most other books. As well as writing about the findings of the science of learning, we designed the book to reflect these findings. So for example, we have mixed up the order of topics as recommended in **Study #4**. We have combined pictures and words **(Study #41)** and asked key questions at the start of most of them **(Study #69)**.

If you do want to read the studies on a particular area, then the topics that we cover are colour-coded as follows:

Memory
Strategies that improve how much students remember things.

Mindset, Motivation and Resilience
How to improve persistence, effort and attitude.

Self-Regulation and Metacognition
Helping students to think clearly, helpfully and consistently.

Student Behaviours
The key student habits and processes that make a meaningful difference.

Teacher Attitudes, Expectations and Behaviours
Important classroom practices that affect student learning.

Parents
The fundamental choices, decisions and behaviours that parents make and how they impact their children's learning.

Thinking Biases
The faulty thinking habits and quirks that get in the way of learning taking place.

Studies

THE ONE ABOUT MEMORY

@inner_drive | www.innerdrive.co.uk

THE STUDY

In 2013, researchers from Kent State University, Duke University, University of Wisconsin and University of Virginia published a review of hundreds of studies to explore which strategies are most likely to lead to long-term learning.

THE MAIN FINDINGS

1 Two techniques were rated as being very effective for improving long-term memory:

Retrieval practice: Students have to generate answers to questions. This includes past papers, multiple choice questions or doing practice essay answers.

Distributed practice: Sometimes referred to as "spacing"; doing little bits of work often instead of a lot all at once (i.e. cramming). Essentially, students remember more if they spread out their learning and revisit the same material across multiple sessions.

2 Two techniques were found to be fairly effective:

Elaborative interrogation: Asking yourself "why is this true?" or "why might this be the case?" This helps students think about the material and make connections with previously learnt information.

Interleaved practice: Interleaving is where students mix up the types of problems they answer, so as to avoid "blocking" their time on just one type of question.

3 Two techniques were found not to be very helpful:

Highlighting/Underlining: Despite being the *weapon of choice* for many students, highlighting material often fails to lead to long-term learning.

Re-reading: Although students may feel that they have learnt something if they can point to a whole chapter that they have read, this may not be as beneficial as they think.

Ref: Dunlosky et al, 2013, *Association for Psychological Science*

THE ONE ABOUT MEMORY

 ## RELATED RESEARCH

Numerous researchers from around the world have run studies that support these findings. For retrieval practice to be most effective, it has to be done at 'low stakes', which means it does not increase stress levels of students and is not used as a form of judgement of their abilities. We still do not know the optimum time to space sessions for distributed practice, which is something currently being explored.

There is evidence to suggest that many students actually prefer to use study strategies that are less likely to lead to better learning. For example, several studies (#23, #88) have found that students were most likely to rate simply re-reading the core material as more helpful than other, more-effective strategies, such as doing lots of quizzes and tests, even though re-reading led to lower exam results. Likewise, many students continue to revise whilst listening to music, even though this does not help (#17).

CLASSROOM IMPLICATIONS

How can teachers use these findings? It will vary depending on the nature of your cohort and the subject you teach. The testing effect can be harnessed through short quizzes at the start or end of a lesson. Likewise, distributed practice is important in education systems in which students no longer do modular exams (such as in the UK), so revisiting previous topics is even more important.

It is important that we teach our students what does and doesn't work. Each minute spent highlighting or re-reading is 60 seconds not spent doing something more effective. As the authors of this study state:

> A premium is placed on teaching students content and critical-thinking skills, whereas less time is spent teaching students to develop effective techniques and strategies to guide learning . . . teaching students to use these techniques would not take much time away from teaching content and would likely be most beneficial if the use of the techniques was consistently taught across multiple content areas, so that students could broadly experience their effects on learning and class grades.

THE ONE ABOUT ASPIRATIONS & EXPECTATIONS

@inner_drive | www.innerdrive.co.uk

THE STUDY

Aspirations are not the same as expectations. The former is what you want to happen, whereas the latter is what you expect to happen. But how much impact does having high aspirations and expectations have on student performance? Does telling a student to reach for the stars make them more likely to do so?

Researchers from Bristol University tracked 770 students from over 640 schools to see if their aspirations and expectations affected their GCSE results and if they went on to apply to University.

THE MAIN FINDINGS

1 **Most students** (58%) have both high aspirations and expectations.

2 Students with **low aspirations and low expectations did the worst** at GCSEs, with those with **higher aspirations and expectations** getting, on average, **2 more GCSEs** graded A*–C.

58%

3 Having **high aspirations and low expectations** often led to **low achievement**. These students were twice as likely to get less than 5 GCSE's at A*–C than their peers who had both high aspirations and expectations.

4 Students whose **parents expected them to go to University** when they were in Year 9 were **over 5 times more likely** to do so than the students whose parents did not.

Ref: Khattab, 2015, *British Educational Research Journal*

THE ONE ABOUT ASPIRATIONS AND EXPECTATIONS

RELATED RESEARCH

Subsequent research has found that most aspiration interventions do little to improve educational attainment. Having high aspirations but being unable to achieve them has been found to result in student resentment, frustration and social withdrawal.

The research has been far more positive on the impact and predictive power of high expectations if combined with high aspirations. Having high expectations of themselves has been found to help students have the confidence to answer more questions correctly on a quiz. Research suggests that having high expectations is most beneficial if done at the start of the school year or at the beginning of a new project, as this allows students to approach it with no negative preconceptions or ideas.

An interesting related area of research has focused on the impact that parental and teacher expectations have on student performance. In most cases, this has been found to help raise student performance (#9, #11). A word of caution though: if expectations are too high and unrealistic, then this can lead to an increase in stress and anxiety (#33).

CLASSROOM IMPLICATIONS

This study suggests that having high aspirations and expectations are important. However, interventions targeting all students may be unsuccessful as many of them already have high levels of both. Programmes targeting selected students who have low aspirations and expectations would likely yield far better results for the time, energy and cost that they would require.

Another approach would be to work with students who already have high aspirations but have low expectations. As the authors of the study note:

> The data that has been presented here suggests that policy makers, teachers and other professionals in schools should encourage their students to raise and maintain high levels of aspirations. However, these high aspirations should be reinforced by equipping students, particularly those coming from poor and disadvantaged families, with necessary skills.

These skills include any that help harness the motivation that comes with having high aspirations that can be turned into better grades. These include strategies such as metacognition, self-regulation and effective memory strategies such as spacing and retrieval practice and teaching the material to someone else (#42).

THE ONE ABOUT THE PLANNING FALLACY

@inner_drive | www.innerdrive.co.uk

THE STUDY

The Planning Fallacy states that most people underestimate how long a task will take to complete. Keen to see if this applies to students, researchers asked pupils to predict how long various pieces of course work and activities would take them to complete. They then measured how accurate the students were and under which conditions they were most likely to achieve their predictions.

THE MAIN FINDINGS

1 Over **70%** of students **finished their assignment later** than they had predicted they would, with the average time taken being over **55 days** compared to the average prediction of **34 days**.

2 Students **took longer to finish the activity than they predicted** regardless of the nature of the task, be it an academic piece of work or everyday activity, such as cleaning their apartment or fixing their bike.

HOW LONG YOU THINK IT WILL TAKE →

HOW LONG IT WILL TAKE →

3 **58%** of students who spent time **actively recalling similar previous tasks** were accurate in predicting how long the next task would take.

Students **who did not use** this technique were only accurate **29%** of the time.

4 Students were more likely to **finish a task on time** if the deadline **was set for them**, rather than setting one themselves.

5 When making future predictions, students were **more likely to think about their future progress** instead of potential future obstacles.

Ref: Buehler, Griffin and Ross, 1994, *Journal of Personality and Social Psychology*

THE ONE ABOUT THE PLANNING FALLACY

RELATED RESEARCH

There has been a lot of research on the importance of setting goals and deadlines and knowing how long is left in a task (#95). Setting goals can help students focus their attention, minimise distractions and enhance work ethic and persistence. Likewise, setting regular deadlines has been found to help students manage their time and energy over the course of the year as well as improve their overall grades (#56). This is because the further away a deadline seems, the less impact it has on people's attention, which subsequently reduces how effectively they spread out their efforts.

Other research to help people better manage their time has revolved around minimising procrastination. One popular strategy to do this includes just doing the task for a few minutes, as actually starting a new project is half the battle. Other techniques include improving self-regulation so that students are less likely to get distracted, as well as doing the hard and important tasks early in the day, as they probably have more energy than compared to late at night.

CLASSROOM IMPLICATIONS

As students get older, there is more of an emphasis on independent study. Clearly, managing students' time is an important skill needed for this, as is making accurate estimations on how long different tasks will take.

Results from this study suggest that there are two key things that teachers can do to better help students make more-accurate predictions. The first is to break a task down and set short regular deadlines. The second is to help students make clear, explicit comparisons to previous similar tasks they have done. Helping them draw similarities and distinguish differences, as well as reflecting on how long these tasks took, will help improve their planning time.

The researchers of this study offer a word of warning on this, though, noting that "it seems that people can know the past and yet still be doomed to repeat it". Teachers can play a key role in helping their students learn from their previous mistakes. Indeed, the researchers state that "individuals will generate more realistic and accurate predictions if they take past completion times into account. This improvement in prediction should only occur, however, if participants' recollections are valid and if their present task is comparable with the projects that they recall". Teachers are well placed to offer guidance and provide a sense of perspective on this.

THE ONE ABOUT SPACING YOUR LEARNING

@inner_drive | www.innerdrive.co.uk

THE STUDY

Researchers devised an experiment to explore the optimum amount of time to leave between revision sessions.

They had 1,354 students learn 32 obscure but true trivia facts. These included questions such as "who invented snow golf?" and "which European nation consumes the most spicy Mexican food?". They then divided the participants into 26 groups, each with a different gap before their next revision session and a different amount of time after that before their final test. They then compared how many successful answers the participants recorded in their final exam to determine the optimum amount of time to leave between study sessions.

THE MAIN FINDINGS

✓ **Spacing is more effective than cramming.**

✓ **The optimum gap to leave before you revisit the same material depends on how long you want to remember the material.**

✓ **The further away the test, the longer the gaps between study sessions should be.**

The researchers found the following timings offer a good guideline:

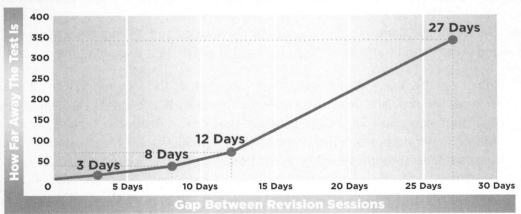

Ref: Cepeda et al, 2008, *Psychological Science*

THE ONE ABOUT SPACING YOUR LEARNING

RELATED RESEARCH

The Spacing Effect is one of the longest and most enduring findings in cognitive psychology. It was first detailed in 1885 by German psychologist Hermann Ebbinghaus, who found that humans tend to forget large amounts of information if they only learn something once. This is partially why students suffer from a "summer learning loss" over the school holidays (#94). Since Ebbinghaus, research has consistently shown the power of spacing out your learning (#66). This is an effective technique, as it allows time for the material to be forgotten and relearnt. This process can help a student cement this knowledge into their long-term memory.

In some studies, using spacing instead of cramming has resulted in a 10-30% difference in final test results. This finding has been found in a range of tasks, including remembering key words, random facts or solving complex maths problems.

The gap between study sessions listed in this study offer a guideline only, as other research recommends slightly different gaps. The researchers of this study state that "to put it simply, if you want to know the optimal distribution of your study time, you need to decide how long you wish to remember something". As a rough rule of thumb, the closer you are to forgetting a piece of information (before it completely drops out of your brain), the more likely it is that you will benefit from revisiting it.

CLASSROOM IMPLICATIONS

The ability to retain and recall large pieces of information has become even more important for students. Teachers can help students improve their long-term memory by spacing out the material and revisiting it regularly. Just as actors don't leave all their rehearsals until the day before the opening night of a play, and athletes don't only train the day before the match, so students should regularly return to previously learnt material.

The authors of this study note that this is "at odds with many conventional educational practices - for example, study of a single topic being confined within a given week of a course". To commit something to memory, it takes time and repetition. This is something for students to carefully consider when making revision timetables, as it is not just the "what" that matters, but the "when" as well.

THE ONE ABOUT GROWTH MINDSET

@inner_drive | www.innerdrive.co.uk

THE STUDY

Students aged 9–12 completed a problem-solving game and were then told that they had gotten 80% of the questions right. Some of them were praised for their natural intelligence, whereas others were praised for how hard they had worked. The researchers investigated how the students felt, thought and behaved in subsequent tasks.

THE MAIN FINDINGS

1 Children who had been praised for their **intelligence** were more likely to choose future tasks that they thought would make them **look smart**. Children who had been praised for their **effort** tended to choose tasks that would help them **learn new things**.

2 Children who had been praised for their intelligence said that they **enjoyed the task less**, when compared to the children who had been praised for their effort.

3 Children who had been praised for their intelligence were **less likely to persist on tasks** than the children who had been praised for their effort.

4 Children who had been praised for their intelligence **performed worse** in future tasks. The children who had been praised for their effort **performed better** in future tasks.

5 86% of children who had been praised for their intelligence asked for information about how their peers did on the same task. Only **23% of children** who had been praised for effort asked for this type of feedback, with the majority of them asking for feedback about what they could do better.

6 38% of children who had been praised for ability lied about the number of problems they solved in the task. Only **13% of the children** praised for effort did.

Ref: Mueller and Dweck, 1998, *The Journal of Personality and Social Psychology*

THE ONE ABOUT GROWTH MINDSET

 ## RELATED RESEARCH

Since this study, many different researchers have studied the impact of having a growth mindset. Some, though certainly not all, have found that having a growth mindset leads to better grades. This effect seems especially true for students who have previously struggled with their studies. Away from exam results, research suggests that having a growth mindset has many other advantages. These include coping better with transitions (#68, #81) and higher self-regulation, grit, positive social behaviour and using more effective revision techniques (#88).

Another fascinating area of growth mindset research is on the associated mental health benefits, with evidence suggesting those with a growth mindset are less aggressive, have higher self-esteem and have less depressive and anxious symptoms.

CLASSROOM IMPLICATIONS

This study highlights the complexities and importance of how we deliver feedback. Too much praise can lead to narcissistic behaviour and create a culture of low expectation. The problem with praise such as "you are so clever" or "you must be so talented" is that it does not tell students what they need to do in the future in order to be successful. By praising their effort and/or the strategies they used, we give students a template of behaviours that they can follow next time.

The study authors, from Columbia and Stanford University, comment that "children exposed to this intelligence feedback, with an emphasis on proving ability through high performance, were likely to respond negatively when they faced achievement setbacks . . . children given effort feedback, on the other hand, who valued learning over performance, were understandably less likely to fall apart when they experienced an isolated low performance". Studies like this must make us consider the merit of calling certain students "gifted and talented" as it implies to them that it is their gifts and talents that will make them successful, not what they do with it (#10). Interestingly, evidence suggests this type of praise may also lead to an increased likelihood of students cheating to maintain this smart reputation (#57).

In the rush to embrace growth mindset, sometimes the message behind the research has been either diluted into "growth mindset is all about effort" or morphed into "anyone can do anything". Neither of these statements are accurate or helpful. Having a growth mindset is about the belief that someone can learn and improve.

THE ONE ABOUT PREDICTING FUTURE BEHAVIOUR

@inner_drive | www.innerdrive.co.uk

THE STUDY

Once a year, over four days in spring at Cornell University, students are encouraged to buy a daffodil. All the money raised goes to the charity American Cancer Society. To help boost sales, access to daffodils is easy, as the campus is flooded with them, they do not cost much and students are made aware of the good cause that the proceeds will go to.

A month before the daffodils were due to go on sale, researchers asked 251 students if they were planning to buy a daffodil and if so, how many they would purchase. Three days after the event, the same students were again surveyed in order to find out how many they actually bought.

THE MAIN FINDINGS

Before the daffodil drive

83% of students said that they would buy a daffodil. They pledged to buy an average of 2 daffodils. Interestingly, these students rated themselves as being more likely to buy a daffodil than their classmates.

After the daffodil drive

When the researchers questioned the whole cohort of pupils after the event, they found that only **43%** of the students had bought a daffodil.

Students also bought fewer daffodils than expected. The average purchase was 1.2 daffodils as opposed to the 2 they had predicted.

Why are we bad at guessing our future behaviour?
Perhaps when predicting what will happen, we are more likely to think of ourselves and the situation with rose-tinted glasses. We are unlikely to accurately consider the obstacles and effort required. This means that students may have good intentions with their work, but may not always convert these good intentions into actions by themselves.

Ref: Epley and Dunning, 2000, *Journal of Personality and Social Psychology*

THE ONE ABOUT PREDICTING FUTURE BEHAVIOUR

 ## RELATED RESEARCH

Other research has confirmed that individuals are quite bad at predicting future behaviours, especially ones that will make us happier (#86). Evidence suggests that to make accurate predictions, we should take the average of a group. This is called "the wisdom of crowds". Surveying a group and taking the average helps to reduce self-serving biases and removes extreme outliers.

In terms of helping turn good intentions into action, creating a productive environment for behavioural change seems to be a powerful technique. This means minimising potential distractions for procrastination, increasing autonomy and tapping into intrinsic motivation by making things fun, mastering the task or creating a sense of purpose. These have all been found to help boost positive change.

CLASSROOM IMPLICATIONS

So if students are not very good at predicting their future behaviour, how can we best support students in the classroom - especially when, as students get older, being an independent learner is more important? As well as taking future predictions with a pinch of salt, it is important to remember that these failed predictions are not necessarily caused by students lying - in this study, the pupils really did believe they would buy lots of daffodils.

Harnessing your students' energy whilst also planning what obstacles they may face and how they will overcome them seems key. It is not negative to talk about what may go wrong, as long as it is followed up with productive discussion about what to do in such an eventuality. This model of "if this, then I'll do that" is a subtle yet powerful strategy to help convert good intentions into actual behaviour.

THE ONE ABOUT TEACHER MINDSET

@inner_drive | www.innerdrive.co.uk

THE STUDY

Researchers ran a series of studies to explore the impact that a teacher's mindset had on their students. They asked trainee teachers to imagine that one of their students had attained a poor mark in a maths exam (65%). The teachers were then surveyed on their view of their student's ability and how they would respond to that student. The researchers then created a scenario from these reactions and asked students how these responses would make them feel.

THE MAIN FINDINGS

1 Teachers with a fixed mindset were **over one-third more likely to view the poor exam result as proof that the student lacked maths ability** when compared to those with a growth mindset.

2 Teachers with a fixed mindset **were more likely to endorse a comfort-focused approach** to these students, with the intention of making the student feel better (i.e. "don't worry, not everyone can be good at maths").

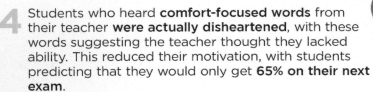

3 Teachers **with a growth mindset were more likely to endorse a strategy-focused approach** to these students. This included tangible ways they could improve and asking them questions in class so that they could practise.

4 Students who heard **comfort-focused words** from their teacher **were actually disheartened**, with these words suggesting the teacher thought they lacked ability. This reduced their motivation, with students predicting that they would only get **65% on their next exam**.

5 Students who had heard **strategy-focused words** from their teacher had an **increase in their motivation**, with them predicting that they would be able to use these strategies to get around **80% on their next exam**.

Ref: Rattan et al, 2012, *Journal of Experimental Social Psychology*

THE ONE ABOUT TEACHER MINDSET

RELATED RESEARCH

Surprisingly, there is not a lot of other research on the impact that the mindset of an adult has on their students. One experiment in England found that teaching teachers about growth mindset had little impact on student performance, although a recent one from America did find a positive impact.

Another study (#16) found that if a parent had a fixed or growth mindset, this had little impact on their child's performance. What mattered more was how the parents reacted to failures and setbacks. Someone's mindset is not always visible to others. It is hard to accurately guess someone's beliefs. What is easier to see is their actions.

It stands to reason that the same is probably true for teachers. Students may not be able to accurately infer their teacher's mindset, but they can accurately assess their actions. The rollercoaster that is the school year is comprised of a series of highs and lows for students. How teachers react to their lows will impact their motivation and how they view themselves. It appears that having a growth mindset is important, but in itself, it may not be enough. It is the doing that matters.

CLASSROOM IMPLICATIONS

Having high expectations that all your students can improve is central to good teaching. Despite having good intentions, the comfort-focused approach of telling students that "not everyone can be good at maths" appears to do more harm than good, as it conveys a sense of low expectations and suggests that they will forever be stuck with their low abilities. This is a classic example of the difference between what the teacher says and what the student hears.

A teacher's mindset shapes their teaching practices, which in turn can affect how students seem themselves. If you want to accelerate this process, there are some guidelines that may be helpful for teachers to know. These include focusing on strategy and providing a step-by-step guide. Nothing will make students feel better than mastering something they have previously been unable to do. In the short term, focusing on strategy may be more painful than the comfort-focused approach, but, in the long term, it is worth the reward.

THE ONE ABOUT TEENAGERS AND SOCIAL REJECTION

@inner_drive | www.innerdrive.co.uk

THE STUDY

Having to navigate the teenage years whilst learning and performing in school can be a real challenge for our students. Keen to test if they are less immune to social rejection than adults, researchers ran a fascinating study in 2010.

They had young teenagers, old teenagers and adults play an electronic game of catch. In a virtual online room, they were one of three players. Unbeknownst to them, the other two players were automatic bots playing to a set programme. To start with, the other two bots would include the participants by throwing the ball to them. Other times, they would exclude them, by only playing with each other. The researchers then compared how the participants thought and felt as a result.

THE MAIN FINDINGS

The researchers found that being socially rejected made all three groups feel worse. However, they also found that being excluded from their peer group had the following impact:

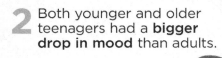

1 Both the younger and older teenagers felt **much worse** than the adults did.

2 Both younger and older teenagers had a **bigger drop in mood** than adults.

3 Younger teenagers had the **biggest increase in anxiety**.

4 Older teenagers had generally **lower self-esteem** than adults.

Ref: Sebastian et al, 2010, *Brain and Cognition*

THE ONE ABOUT TEENAGERS AND SOCIAL REJECTION

 ## RELATED RESEARCH

The authors of this study, from University College London and Purdue University, noted that their findings "suggest that teenagers are hypersensitive to rejection" and also stated that their findings "are in line with previous work showing that social anxiety is at its peak at age 15". This effect may be particularly pronounced in teenage girls, with one study finding that girls suffer a significant decrease in self-esteem during their teenage years.

We now know more about the teenage brain than we ever did before. It is structured and functions differently than an adult's brain. Other research has demonstrated how teenagers are more likely to take risks, need more sleep, struggle to read emotions and have less self-control than adults. Although we are all susceptible to peer pressure (#73), evidence suggests that teenagers are more likely to be influenced by the group and are more likely than adults to make bad decisions when in the company of their friends.

CLASSROOM IMPLICATIONS

A person will never be surrounded by so many people their own age than when they are at school. If teenagers are more sensitive to social rejection than adults, then navigating their teenage years at school presents a tricky tightrope for them. Excessive levels of stress can hinder learning, concentration and memory, meaning that what happens out on the playground (and also online on social media after school) can affect what happens in the classroom. Therefore, it is important that we explicitly teach students strategies that help them manage their anxieties and frustrations. This includes techniques such as self-talk (#53), deep breathing, refocusing and reframing.

It is also interesting to note the different reactions that teenagers and adults had in this study. This shows how two people can experience the same event and have very different reactions. This does not mean that teenagers are over-reacting when they experience social rejection. At this stage of their life, social standing is an important currency. Finding a balance between empathising with them whilst also putting the latest slight into perspective is crucial.

THE ONE ABOUT TEACHER EXPECTATIONS

@inner_drive | www.innerdrive.co.uk

THE STUDY

Researchers falsely told teachers that some of their students had been identified as potential high achievers and that they would bloom over the course of the year. These students were in fact chosen at random. The researchers then went back at the end of the school year to find out how these students had got on.

THE MAIN FINDINGS

1 The students that were chosen were more likely to make **larger gains in their academic performance** over the course of the year than the control group.

The researchers attributed this to their teachers having **high expectations** of them and subsequently altering their behaviours.

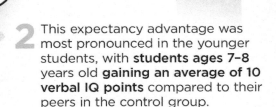

2 This expectancy advantage was most pronounced in the younger students, with **students ages 7–8 years old gaining an average of 10 verbal IQ points** compared to their peers in the control group.

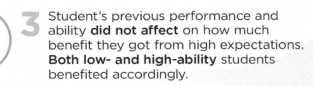

3 Student's previous performance and ability **did not affect** on how much benefit they got from high expectations. **Both low- and high-ability** students benefited accordingly.

4 The most significant benefit for male students came with an increase in **verbal IQ**, with girls mainly benefiting from an increase in **reasoning IQ**.

Ref: Rosenthal and Jacobson, 1966, *The Urban Review*

THE ONE ABOUT TEACHER EXPECTATIONS

RELATED RESEARCH

In Greek mythology, Pygmalion was a renowned sculptor who fell in love with an ivory statue he had carved. He loved his statue so much that Aphrodite, the goddess of love, turned it into a real-life being. The Pygmalion effect is the name given to the phenomenon of people achieving and living up to someone else's high standards.

The opposite of the Pygmalion effect is the "Golem Effect". This describes how having low expectations can lead to either self-handicapping behaviours or a self-fulfilling prophecy, in which students fail because they and/or their teachers do not believe that they will succeed.

It is also important to distinguish between aspirations and expectations. Aspirations are about wanting to be better, whereas expectations convey a belief about the likelihood of succeeding. Research suggests (#2) that students in England who have high aspirations but low expectations are twice as likely to get fewer than five GCSEs at A*-C. The disconnect occurs in the gap between having these high ambitions and the daily behaviours and habits required to achieve them.

CLASSROOM IMPLICATIONS

No-one rises to low expectations. Having high expectations of each student, and then providing the necessary support needed to achieve those expectations, seems key to raising student achievement. As the authors of this study noted, "when teachers expected that certain children would show greater intellectual development, those children did show greater intellectual development".

How can a teacher tangibly demonstrate their high expectations for their students? Possible strategies include expecting all students to contribute, having consistently high standards and varying support to students instead of lowering expectations of what they can achieve. Furthermore, taking time to verbalise your high expectations for students and explaining that you believe in them and that you will work hard with them to help them achieve these goals will help drive an increase in standards and in their self-belief.

THE ONE ABOUT IQ AND SUCCESS

@inner_drive | www.innerdrive.co.uk

THE STUDY

How much of a child's success is down to their IQ? Do genes dictate success? And can you accurately predict which of your students are going to go on to be successful?

Dr. Lewis Terman was responsible for one of the largest ongoing longitudinal studies on gifted and talented students. Based at Stanford University in the 1920s, he initially believed that a person's IQ would determine their success. Their success both in school and subsequently in adult life were monitored (and still continue to be today).

The children in his study often affectionately referred to themselves as the "Termites". Dr. Terman believed that his 'termites' would go on to be the leaders of their generation due to their genius-like IQ scores. The data is updated roughly every five years. As a result, we now know more than ever how important IQ is and what other factors determine success in both school and in life.

THE MAIN FINDINGS

As expected, the termite students went on to do very well at school. What is most interesting about this study is the results of the follow-up studies on these students.

After 25 years, Dr. Terman started comparing the type of career his termites had taken up. Some were doctors, lawyers and university professors. Others were filing clerks, policeman or fisherman. Surprised at the wide range, Terman famously commented that "we have seen that intellect and achievement are far from perfectly correlated".

Thirty-five years after his initial study, Dr. Terman compared the 100 most successful participants (referred to as As) with those who were struggling at age 40 (referred to as Cs). They found that:

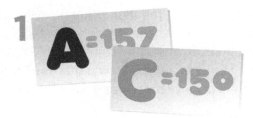

The As did indeed have a higher IQ than the Cs (157 versus 150), but concluded that this was not very significant, as **small differences between high IQ** have little real-life impact.

One of the most important differences between the two groups was **their character traits**. From a young age, the Cs showed a lack of determination and persistence, whereas the As already showed greater "will power, perseverance and desire to excel".

Ref: Terman, 1925, *Genetic Studies of Genius*

THE ONE ABOUT IQ AND SUCCESS

RELATED RESEARCH

The "Termite Study" offers a fascinating insight into the predictive power of IQ. Other research has confirmed that a person's IQ has a large genetic component and is highly correlated with their academic performance, creativity, happiness, future earnings and even life expectancy. Clearly, IQ plays a significant role in our lives.

Other research has highlighted the importance of mindset, resilience, emotional intelligence and grit towards success (#14). This has been associated with how well students cope with change, how they recover from setbacks and how they process feedback. Research has found that it is clearly not a case of nature versus nurture but a combination of both. The important question is not "which has most impact?" but "which areas can we help improve?" and "how do we best do so?". Research on this is ongoing and is unlikely to ever reach a definitive answer.

CLASSROOM IMPLICATIONS

This study, along with others (#22), raises some interesting questions, namely: how good are we at predicting who is going to be successful? And how do we best nurture the skills that will help them to do well? Evidence suggests that in primary schools, high achievement is often due to date of birth, with students born in the early months of the academic year having a massive advantage over their younger peers. What we think of as "talent" and "intelligence" in the early years may actually just be age-related.

Indeed, given the time taken to predict grades and future outcomes, it is worth considering if predicting grades and future outcomes really helps. On the plus side, it can be used to track progress and ensure that students are getting the right level of support. However, it is worth considering the opportunity cost as each minute spent predicting the future is 60 seconds not spent helping students learn.

THE ONE ABOUT PARENTS AND GRADES

@inner_drive | www.innerdrive.co.uk

THE STUDY

It is one of the most common and important questions that parents ask teachers at parents evening–"what can I do to best help support my child?". So researchers reviewed 37 studies on the effects of parental behaviours and attitudes on childrens' grades. This involved a sample of over 80,000 students and their families. They then made suggestions as to what does and doesn't work.

THE MAIN FINDINGS

Their study found that four of the best things a parent can do at primary and secondary school level to help their child's grades are:

1 Have high academic expectations
Having high aspirations and expectations of your child **has the biggest impact** on their grades. Parental expectations include how important school is, their attitude towards teachers, and the value of education.

2 Regular communication
This includes developing and maintaining communication with children about their school life. This **helps parents nip any potential problems** in the bud before they manifest into bigger issues.

3 Good reading habits
This involves **reading frequently and regularly with your child**. This includes reading to them and encouraging them to read alongside you as well.

4 Homework rules
This revolves around having clear rules to deal with how they divide their homework and leisure time. Explaining why these rules are in place **can help them to make better decisions** regarding their independent study time later in their school career.

By contrast they found that behaviours such as parental attendance of school activities and supervising homework did not make a significant impact on grades.

Ref: Castro et al, 2015, *Infant and Child Development*

THE ONE ABOUT PARENTS AND GRADES

RELATED RESEARCH

A large body of research has confirmed the findings of this study, specifically, the power of high expectations and valuing education (#85). This impact has been found when those expectations come from parents, teachers or the students themselves.

Likewise, developing good reading habits and reading for pleasure has also been associated with improvements in vocabulary, spelling, maths and general academic achievements. Given its importance, it is a worry that in 2016 the National Literacy Trust reported that only 40% of teenagers enjoyed reading, and only 24% said that reading was "cool".

The study finding that it is important to have clear rules around homework time is interesting, as other research has found that students who do their homework themselves (i.e. without parental supervision) do better (#67). This is because, when students get older, their homework becomes more complex, and then they need to take individual responsibility and ownership for their own success.

CLASSROOM IMPLICATIONS

The authors of the study note that "anyone concerned about education would like to know which malleable variables have the greatest effect on educational performance. But, unfortunately, it seems that the largest effects are associated with variables outside the scope of administrators or policy makers". How much influence can schools have on these important factors? We may not be able to determine parental behaviours and attitudes, but we can do our best to influence them.

Educating parents is important. Parents have limited knowledge from a small sample size of what does and doesn't work (i.e. their own experiences with their children). Schools and teachers have a wide, varied and deep experience base of helping students achieve educational success. It therefore stands to reason that part of the role and responsibility of a school is to transmit and transfer this knowledge. Parent evenings, evening workshops and newsletters are great ways to communicate this information to parents.

THE ONE ABOUT STUDENT RESILIENCE

@inner_drive | www.innerdrive.co.uk

THE STUDY

Calvin Coolidge, the 30th President of the United States of America, once noted that "nothing in this world can take the place of persistence. Talent will not; nothing is more common than unsuccessful men with talent. Genius will not; unrewarded genius is almost a proverb. Education will not; the world is full of educated derelicts. Persistence and determination alone are omnipotent". Whilst he might have been slightly over-exaggerating the importance of resilience, the desire to help students improve these skills is probably more popular now than ever. But is resilience something that can be learnt and developed?

Resilience, originally studied in young children suffering major traumatic events, has since been researched in both sport and business. A recent study has now turned the focus to resilience in education. Through interviews with students, researchers identified three key attributes that lead to resilient learners, as well as suggested what academic institutions can do to help facilitate their development.

THE MAIN FINDINGS

Researchers found three key attributes behind resilience:

A sense of perspective
This included managing one's emotions, concentrating on things one can control and setting both short- and long-term goals. Central to maintaining a sense of perspective was the importance of self-reflection, which allowed students to manage new or uncomfortable situations.

Staying healthy
This helped students respond well under pressure and during adversity. Ways to do this included doing physical activity and participating in team sports, which prompted more social interactions. Identifying and celebrating successes and positive self-talk helped improve mental well-being.

Social support
The more someone isolates themselves, the more likely they are to brood over bad decisions. Maintaining good relationships with friends, family and teachers helps students either feel better about their setbacks and/or provides suggestions on how they can possibly overcome them.

Finally, the study looked at what academic institutions could do to help foster resilient environments for their students. They found that helping them experience and learn from failures in a safe environment, providing high-quality feedback that focuses on strategies and next steps, as well as access to extra-curricular activities, helped.

Ref: Holdsworth et al, 2017, *Studies in Higher Education*

THE ONE ABOUT STUDENT RESILIENCE

RELATED RESEARCH

This study supports existing research that has found that resilience is something that can be developed by the individual as well as facilitated by their environment (#62). A recent overview (#39) by leading resilience researchers highlighted that for an environment to facilitate resilience it needs to be both high in challenge and support. Too much challenge and no support results in excessive stress, burnout and isolation. Too much support but not enough challenge can lead to complacency and boredom.

Other strategies that have been found to help improve resilience include being open to new experiences, being optimistic, viewing decisions as active choices instead of sacrifices and focusing on developing one's skills instead of comparing oneself to others. Viewing setbacks as opportunities for learning as well as taking personal responsibility for one's own thoughts and feelings will help.

Research has also demonstrated that setbacks and struggling are not always a bad thing (#74). Those who have experienced some adversity tend to perform better under pressure in the future than those who have been wrapped in cotton wool. Experiencing failure has also been associated with higher levels of empathy, motivation and determination.

CLASSROOM IMPLICATIONS

The authors of this study note that "failure is a central part of learning, but its associated connotations need to be reconceptualised as a learning opportunity". Many students feel that:

mistakes = bad = avoid at all costs

Helping them understand that mistakes and setbacks at some stage are inevitable, and then providing them with strategies to capitalise on the mistakes, will help us develop resilient learners.

Taking time to talk to students about how to improve both their physical and mental well-being will help equip them with the energy and skills needed to navigate tough times. Likewise, teaching students skills such as self-reflection and how to set appropriate goals will benefit them.

THE ONE ABOUT MARSHMALLOWS AND SELF-CONTROL

@inner_drive | www.innerdrive.co.uk

THE STUDY

If I offered you a marshmallow and told you that if you refrained from eating it for 15 minutes, I would give you two instead, would you be able to do it? In the early 1970s, researchers asked 92 3- to 5-year-olds this question. The original study and the follow-up studies 20 years later changed how we viewed self-control forever.

This study is important for teachers to know. Firstly, it is so simple that you could easily replicate it yourself (and many have). Secondly, it is a longitudinal study, which means we get to track the path of the students in the study over many years. Third and finally, it is one of the most famous studies in psychology and is a staple in most psychology and education handbooks.

THE MAIN FINDINGS

Some students, when given the choice between **eating a marshmallow straight away** or **waiting to get two marshmallows later**, could barely contain themselves and ate the first marshmallow straight away.

Other students were able to wait and delay their gratification, and as a result were able to get the sweet, sticky reward of the extra marshmallow.

Effective strategies employed by those who exercised better impulse control included distracting themselves from the temptation by thinking about other fun things, closing their eyes or sitting on their hands.

In **follow-up studies**, researchers found that the longer the students waited for their marshmallow as young children, the more likely they were as adults to be:

| More attentive | Socially competent | Academically successful | Verbally fluent | Able to deal with frustration and stress |

It would appear that the ability to delay gratification predicts individual differences in developmental outcomes. It would appear that "self-control is crucial for the successful pursuit of long-term goals. It is equally essential for developing the self-restraint and empathy needed to build caring and mutually supportive relationships".

Ref: Shoda et al, 1990, *Developmental Psychology*

THE ONE ABOUT MARSHMALLOWS AND SELF-CONTROL

RELATED RESEARCH

Subsequent researchers have focused on what causes some children to seek instant gratification and why others are more willing to wait. Some researchers believe it is down to differences in the brain, with those who give in to temptation having less activity in their prefrontal lobes (associated with conscious decision making and impulse control) and more in the ventral striatum (associated with addictive behaviours).

Other researchers think it may be associated with trust, with a different study finding that if young children don't believe they are going to get a second marshmallow if they wait, they are more likely to eat the first one (#31). This has some interesting implications for students who perceive school, teachers or parents as not being trustworthy (#81).

Finally, others have suggested that students who "fail" the marshmallow test may not do so because of limited self-control, but because they are acting very logically. If you grow up with very limited resources around you, it may make sense to take the immediate rewards, as opportunities to do so again in the future may be scarce. A very recent study seemed to support this, noting that a child's background and environment is a better predictor of future outcomes than their ability to delay gratification on the marshmallow task.

CLASSROOM IMPLICATIONS

Is school one big marshmallow test? With an ever-increasing amount of distractions (including, but not limited to, mobile phones), then the ability to improve self-control and delayed gratification has become a premium skill. Perhaps it is not surprising that recent research by the London School of Economics found that schools that have banned mobile phones see an increase in exam results (#49).

Maturity could be described as the increasing gap between thinking something and deciding to act on it. The way the brain develops during the teenage years means that there are significant developments that reduce sensation seeking whilst improving impulse control. As well as removing temptations, having discussions about how to improve self-regulation and delayed gratification, and why students should want to do so, are good starting points.

THE ONE ABOUT MINDSET AND PURPOSE

@inner_drive | www.innerdrive.co.uk

THE STUDY

This study explored the impact of teaching students how to develop a growth mindset (i.e. the belief that I can get better) and a sense of purpose (i.e. why I should care about what I'm doing). Researchers explored what impact these interventions had, if they were scalable, and for which type of student they were most beneficial.

This study was based on 1,594 students from 13 different high schools. Students were either assigned to a control group, a group getting just a growth mindset intervention, a group getting a sense of purpose intervention or a group getting both a growth mindset and a sense of purpose intervention.

These interventions were designed to be brief and delivered online. The growth mindset intervention involved a single 45-minute online session that included information about how the brain develops and how students had potential to become more intelligent through study and practice, as well as having them summarise the key findings in a letter to another student. The sense of purpose intervention had students explain how doing well at school could help them achieve meaningful goals which included "making a positive impact in the world" or "making their family proud".

THE MAIN FINDINGS

1 Students who had a **growth mindset intervention** had an increase in their grades.

2 Students who had a **sense of purpose intervention** had an increase in their grades.

3 Students who had growth mindset and sense of purpose interventions were **more likely to complete** their courses in English, maths and science.

4 The above findings were most pronounced for students who had been identified as **struggling or at risk of dropping** out of school.

5 Both growth mindset and sense of purpose interventions **were found to be scalable**, meaning they could be delivered online to large groups of students.

Ref: Paunesku et al, 2015, *Psychological Science*

THE ONE ABOUT MINDSET AND PURPOSE

RELATED RESEARCH

One fascinating study (#47) looked at creating a sense of purpose for students learning a new foreign language. Some were not given any reason for why they had to learn the material. Others were told they should try hard because it was what was expected of them, whereas others were told there would be a test at the end of the term. Finally, the last group were told that the purpose behind the learning was that it would help their future career. The result? Those who had the explanation as to why learning this new language would be useful to them put in much more effort and were more engaged in the lesson.

Likewise, a range of studies have found that developing a growth mindset may be especially beneficial for struggling students or those who are at risk of dropping out. Some of these studies are worth noting, as their sample size is more than 100,000 students. Other benefits that have been associated with a growth mindset include coping better with transitions, more persistence, self-regulation, well-being, grit and feeling more in control of their lives.

CLASSROOM IMPLICATIONS

This study has clear implications for the classroom as it shows that both a growth mindset and a sense of purpose can be developed quickly and simply. A sense of purpose can be fostered by encouraging students to reflect on how working hard and learning in school can help them accomplish their future goals. This seems to be especially true if these goals involve other people or making the world better. A good starting point would be to have students complete the following sentence: "doing well at school will help me achieve my goals because . . ."

The classroom is also a good place to help develop a growth mindset. Having high expectations that every student can achieve, along with helping them develop a range of strategies that they can call upon following a setback will help. Finally, helping them understand that mistakes can be a useful learning curve and to measure their success against their own high standards, instead of comparing themselves to others, will encourage a growth mindset culture.

THE ONE ABOUT SPACING AND INTERLEAVING

@inner_drive | www.innerdrive.co.uk

THE STUDY

How much impact does the order and timing of questions that students answer have on how well they learn the material? Is spacing, which is doing little and often, better than cramming? Does interleaving, which is mixing up the type of problems, help more than blocking?

In the first study, researchers explored the difference between spacing out maths revision sessions over the course of a week, compared to doing them all in one sitting. In their second study they also measured the impact of working on the same sort of maths problems for the whole session against mixing up the type of questions the students had to answer.

THE MAIN FINDINGS

1 In the final test, students who **spaced out** their revision sessions got an average mark of 74%, whereas those who **crammed** their revision got 49%.

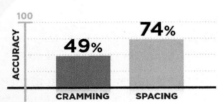

2 One week after their revision, students who interleaved the type of questions they answered got an average of **63%** whilst those that had answered the same sort of problem (i.e. blocking) got on average **20%**

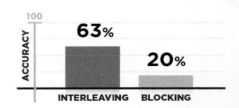

Ref: Rohrer and Taylor, 2007, *Instructional Science*

THE ONE ABOUT SPACING AND INTERLEAVING

 RELATED RESEARCH

There is a lot of research that highlights the benefit of spacing over cramming (#4). Essentially, doing one hour a day for eight days is better than doing eight hours in one day. Other studies have found that using spacing instead of cramming resulted in a 10-30% difference in final test results.

There is also a growing body of evidence that has found that interleaving the types of problems within a subject helps improve long-term retention, recall and performance (#1, #96). This is because this process gives students an opportunity to practice a range of strategies but also the chance to get better at identifying which strategy is most appropriate and likely to succeed. One such study tested children throwing differently weighted bean bags at a target and found that those who mixed up the order of the weights in their practice attempts performed better in the final test than those who practiced with the bean bags in ascending weight order.

CLASSROOM IMPLICATIONS

It is interesting to consider how most maths textbooks describe a problem (i.e. how to add fractions) and then give ten practice questions on that problem. Interleaving may take a bit more time than blocking. The students in this study did better on their mock tests straight after their study session; however, they did not learn it as deeply. This suggests that, for long-term retention, interleaving is far better.

Indeed, the authors of this study note that the benefit of spacing as:

> When practice problems relating to a given topic are spaced across multiple practice sets, a student who fails to understand a lesson (or fails to attend a lesson) will still be able to solve most of the problems within the following practice set, whereas a massed practice set ensures that this student will have little or no success.

Therefore, mixing up the type of problems they face and spacing this out over a large period of time will likely yield far better results.

THE ONE ABOUT PARENTAL VIEWS ON FAILURE

@inner_drive | www.innerdrive.co.uk

THE STUDY

After experiencing a failure, children often look to their parents to see how they react. But what impact does their response have on their child's mindset? Parents can view failure as either "enhancing" or "debilitating". An enhancing view of failure sees setbacks as a chance to learn and grow, whereas a debilitating view of failure sees setbacks as a source of shame and forms the basis of a negative judgement on the child's ability.

Researchers from Stanford University ran a series of studies with over one hundred parent/child pairs in order to explore what impact parental mindsets and their view of failure had on the child's mindset. Their results offer guidance as to how parents can help young students develop a growth mindset (i.e. the belief that one can get better).

THE MAIN FINDINGS

1 Whether a parent had a fixed or a growth mindset **did not predict** their child's mindset.

2 Children **were very accurate** at assessing if their parents viewed failure as either potentially enhancing or debilitating.

3 Parents who **viewed failure as debilitating** were more likely to have a child with a fixed mindset.

4 Parents who **viewed failure as enhancing** were more likely to have a child with a growth mindset.

5 Out of all the parents, older ones were more likely to believe that failure could be **a helpful learning experience**.

As the authors of the study comment, "it may be that parents, like children, have mindsets that shape their own goals and behaviours, but that these beliefs are relevant to shaping children's beliefs only if they lead to practices that children pick up on".

They summarise by stating that "our findings indeed show that parents who believe failure is a debilitating experience have children who believe they cannot develop their intelligence ... these parents react to their children's failures by focusing more on their children's ability or performance than on their learning".

Ref: Haimovitz and Dweck, 2016, *Psychological Science*

THE ONE ABOUT PARENTAL VIEWS ON FAILURE

 RELATED RESEARCH

This study is one of the few that directly looks at how parental beliefs affect and influence their children's mindset. Most of the research to date has looked at how their attitudes affect on student performance (#85), with valuing education and having high but realistic expectations resulting in higher student grades (#11). Other areas to have found similar results include attitude towards homework and positive reading habits. This study is even more pertinent when one considers other research showing the important role failure plays in how someone develops and improves over time (#99).

In terms of developing a growth mindset, other research has focused on parental behaviours instead of attitudes. For example, evidence (#19) suggests that the type of praise parents use when children are very young (ages 1-3) is a significant predictor of their child's mindset up to five years later. Other strategies to help develop a growth mindset include encouraging students to choose challenging tasks, encouraging helpful self-talk and focusing on developing skills instead of comparing oneself to others.

CLASSROOM IMPLICATIONS

The results from this study highlight how someone's mindset may not always be visible to others. It is internal and it is hard to accurately guess someone's beliefs. What is easier to see is their behaviour. This suggests it is not what parents think but what they do that matters. It is not their intentions but their actions that matter. It is totally plausible to assume the same may be true for teachers in the classroom.

Any parents evening or workshop aimed at helping their child develop a growth mindset should include the importance of visibly dealing with setbacks, disappointments and mistakes in a positive way. The researchers conclude by saying:

> It may not be sufficient to teach parents a growth mindset and expect that they will naturally transmit it to their children. Instead, an intervention targeting parents' failure mindset could teach parents how failure can be beneficial, and how to react to their children's setbacks so as to maintain their children's motivation and learning.

This type of intervention not only could lead children to adopt a growth mindset but could also directly help them improve their persistence and resilience by reframing their opinions on failure.

THE ONE ABOUT REVISING TO MUSIC

@inner_drive | www.innerdrive.co.uk

WHY THIS STUDY

Many students do their homework and revision whilst listening to music. Many of these students will swear that listening to their favourite songs helps them study. But does it actually help or hinder learning? And interestingly, does it matter what type of music they listen to whilst revising?

To answer these questions, researchers assigned students of a range of ages to one of four groups; the first revised in silence, the second revised whilst listening to music with lyrics they liked (which included songs from One Direction and Katy Perry), the third group revised to music with lyrics they did not like (which comprised of very heavy thrash metal bands), and the fourth group revised listening to music that did not have lyrics.

The participants then took a test on the passages they had been revising, rating how distracting their environment had been, as well as writing down their predictions for how well they thought they had done.

THE MAIN FINDINGS

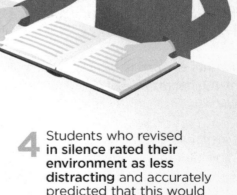

1 Students who revised in **quiet environments performed over 60% better** in an exam than their peers who revised listening to music that had lyrics.

2 Students who revised whilst **listening to music without lyrics did better** than those who had revised to music with lyrics.

3 It made no difference whether students revised listening to songs they **liked or didn't like**. Both led to **a reduction in their subsequent** test performance.

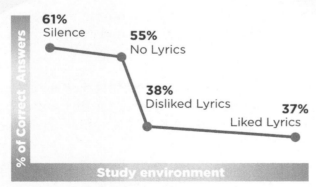

% of Correct Answers

- **61%** Silence
- **55%** No Lyrics
- **38%** Disliked Lyrics
- **37%** Liked Lyrics

Study environment

4 Students who revised **in silence rated their environment as less distracting** and accurately predicted that this would lead to better performances in subsequent tests.

Ref: Perham and Currie, 2014, *Applied Cognitive Psychology*

THE ONE ABOUT REVISING TO MUSIC

 ## RELATED RESEARCH

There are some benefits to listening to music whilst performing certain tasks. It can be quite motivating and can improve mood (i.e. listening to your favourite song tends to make you smile). This is why many people listen to music in the gym. However, evidence suggests that adding music to PowerPoint slides does not translate into learning new or complex material (#78).

The misbelief that music aids learning may stem from a series of studies that have been dubbed "The Mozart Effect". Participants in these studies appeared to be getting smarter and performed better in tests. However, further research has since revealed that this is not the case. Although listening to music before a task can make someone feel better, listening to it whilst trying to learn something new tends not to help. This is because music, especially with lyrics, can take up processing space in the brain. This conflicts with the material you are trying to learn, effectively creating a bottleneck in one's memory, as there is less space to process what you are revising.

The authors of this study, from Cardiff Metropolitan University, are in no doubt when they comment that "despite liking certain lyrical music, it is as detrimental to reading comprehension as listening to disliked music. Music without lyrics was shown to be less detrimental but, expectedly, performing reading comprehension was best in quiet conditions".

CLASSROOM IMPLICATIONS

It is important that students are made aware of the pitfalls of listening to music when studying. What is interesting to note is that this study found that students rated the quiet environment as less distracting and better for them, yet many students will continue to listen to music during their homework. Why would this be the case? Reasons may include doing so out of habit, confusing what improves one's mood with what leads to good learning, alleviating boredom and because everyone else is doing it.

Therefore, students need to know not just what they need to study but how they should study as well. There may well be a time and place to listen to music during their studies, but not when they are learning new and complex material. As the old saying goes, "silence is golden".

THE ONE ABOUT THE DUNNING-KRUGER EFFECT

@inner_drive | www.innerdrive.co.uk

THE STUDY

In 1995, McArthur Wheeler robbed a bank in America in broad daylight. He was surprised later when he was arrested, as he incorrectly believed that covering his face in lemon juice would make him invisible to the CCTV cameras. Inspired by not only his incompetence, but also his lack of awareness, researchers Justin Kruger and David Dunning of Cornell University ran a series of studies to see if lack of ability is linked to low levels of self-awareness.

In their experiments, they had participants perform various tasks and then estimate how well they did. The tasks included telling jokes, logical reasoning and grammar tests. Finally, researchers wanted to see what could be done to help someone more accurately assess their current ability levels.

THE MAIN FINDINGS

1 The **majority of people tend to over-estimate** their abilities. This finding is most pronounced in those with the lowest ability.

2 The level of **over-estimation decreases** the more able the participant is.

3 The Dunning-Kruger effect **has been found in a range of skills** that include logical reasoning, grammar and exam results.

4 The only group of people **who tend to under-estimate** their abilities are the most competent. This is often referred to as **"the burden of expertise"**.

5 Improving someone's metacognitive skills through training and workshops **was found to improve** the accuracy of their self-assessments.

Ref: Kruger and Dunning, 1999, *Journal of Personality and Social Psychology*

THE ONE ABOUT THE DUNNING-KRUGER EFFECT

RELATED RESEARCH

It appears that this research confirms what many notable figures from history have known. Socrates proclaimed that "I know one thing, I know nothing"; Charles Darwin noted that "ignorance more frequently begets confidence than does knowledge"; William Shakespeare in *As You Like It* wrote "the fool doth think he is wise, but the wise man knows himself to be a fool" and Thomas Jefferson once said "he who knows best knows how little he knows". Indeed, Luke Skywalker says in *Star Wars* that overconfidence by the dark side led to the Death Star being blown up.

Why do people not get better at recognising their incompetence, especially if they experience many failures? Research suggests that people may attribute their failures to external factors, such as luck or circumstance, as a way of protecting their self-esteem. This is not a bad short-term strategy to protect confidence, but unfortunately is a poor strategy for long-term learning (#27), especially given how important failure is to one's development (#99).

CLASSROOM IMPLICATIONS

This study has three important classroom implications. Firstly, it is important to be wary of anyone who claims anything with 100% confidence (#43). Indeed, the authors of the study note that "the same incompetence that leads them to make wrong choices also deprives them of the savvy necessary to recognize incompetence, be it their own or anyone else's".

Secondly, it is important that students are aware of their current skill levels if they are going to improve them. If they have over-inflated views of their ability levels (#77), then it is less likely that they are going to reflect on how to improve and get better.

Thirdly, and finally, we have to find a good balance between helping students understand their current level in a way that does not hinder their motivation. If they believe that their abilities are set and not going to change, then they are unlikely to put in additional work. Indeed, research suggests that students with this fixed mindset give up quicker, cope worse with transitions, have poorer coping skills and generally get lower grades.

THE ONE ABOUT PARENTAL PRAISE

@inner_drive | www.innerdrive.co.uk

THE STUDY

Researchers observed the interactions of 53 children aged 1–3 and their parents over a three-year period. During these interactions, the researchers recorded the amount of praise parents gave to their children and categorised it as either "process praise", "person praise" or "other". Process praise focused on the child's effort and strategies, such as "you must have tried really hard there" or "I really liked how you did that". Person praise was defined as praise that centred around a fixed positive quality, such as "you're so smart" or "good girl".

Several years later, when the children were 7–8 years old, the researchers returned to ask the students about their attitude to learning and what motivated them. They then compared the type of praise that the children had received years before to see if there was any correlation.

THE MAIN FINDINGS

1 7- to 8-year-old children who had been praised for their processes, strategies and efforts when aged 1 to 3 were **more likely to have a growth mindset**, embrace challenge, value hard work and be able to generate strategies on how to improve.

2 The type of praise parents use is set **when their children are 14 months old** and remains consistent for the next two years.

24.4%
10.3%

3 Boys and girls both received similar amounts of overall praise, however boys received far more process praise than girls did. **24.4% of praise for boys** was process focused, whereas only **10.3% of praise that girls** received was for their processes. As a result, **boys were more likely** to have a growth mindset five years later.

4 The **mindset of a parent did not necessarily relate** to their child's mindset. What was most closely correlated was the type of praise the parents used. It was those interactions that most influenced their child's mindset.

Ref: Gunderson et al, 2013, *Child Development*

THE ONE ABOUT PARENTAL PRAISE

 ## RELATED RESEARCH

Several other studies suggest that praising a child for their effort and strategies is likely to help them develop a growth mindset and a belief that they can improve (#5). This is because new strategies can be learnt and acquired, thus promoting a more resilient mindset during adversity.

Other studies (#16) have looked to examine the relationship between parental mindset and the child's mindset. Researchers have found that how parents react to their child's setbacks has a significant impact. Those who view them as an opportunity to learn and improve, rather than as negative judgements on their child's ability, are more likely to develop a growth mindset in their children.

The finding in this study, that boys receive more process praise and are thus more likely to have a growth mindset, is an interesting one, as the results from other studies have been mixed. Some report no difference between boys and girls in terms of having a growth mindset, whereas other studies have found that girls are more likely to attribute failure to fixed factors rather than ones that they can change. Some research has also looked at subject-specific mindset and have found that the belief of a limited fixed ability in maths and science is more apparent in young girls than in young boys.

CLASSROOM IMPLICATIONS

The authors of this study, from The University of Chicago and Stanford University, note that "our findings are consistent with the idea that variation in parent praise can impact children's motivational frameworks and that the roots of this impact can be traced back to the toddler years". This would seem to suggest that early education of parents on the impact of the type of praise they use with their children at a young age would be very helpful.

What is also interesting is just how important this parental praise is. Commenting on this, the authors also say that "given that children are likely to receive praise from many adults in their environment, it is remarkable that praise occurring during the thin slices of parent-child interactions [that they observed] provided insight into how children develop [a growth mindset]". Clearly the words children hear from their parents resonate with them long after they have been said.

THE ONE ABOUT EFFORT BEING CONTAGIOUS

@inner_drive | www.innerdrive.co.uk

THE STUDY

How do we get students to work a little bit harder? What impact does the person next to you have on how hard you work? And finally, if they are working hard, does that encourage you to do likewise?

Researchers had 38 students play a reaction-time game on a computer in pairs. Sometimes the tasks were on the same screen, sometimes they were on different screens next to each other. Some of the time they could see what their partner was doing and sometimes they couldn't.

The researchers manipulated the game so that one of the pair had a more difficult task, which forced them to work harder. They then measured what impact this had on the other member of the pair.

THE MAIN FINDINGS

1 Students were **more likely to work harder** on a task if the person next to them was working hard.

2 It did not matter if a student couldn't see **what task the other person was working on**; if the other student was working hard it still encouraged them to do so as well.

Why was this the case?
It may be due to the bandwagon effect, which is when people adopt the behaviours of those around them. Another reason may be due to our automatic need to imitate those around us (i.e. if someone next to you yawns, you are more likely to do the same). Another reason may be that as human beings, we are very aware of other people's thoughts about us and want to make a good impression.

Ref: Desender et al, 2016, *Psychonomic Bulletin & Review*

THE ONE ABOUT EFFORT BEING CONTAGIOUS

RELATED RESEARCH

One of the first studies ever conducted in sport psychology, more than 100 years ago, found that people would cycle faster on a bike machine if they were being observed by others. Building on this, other research found that, if done in front of others, skills that were either simple or well-learnt were performed better.

However, it is not all straightforward. A fascinating study found that each person added to a tug-of-war team resulted in each member putting in less effort. This is known as "social loafing" and is often caused by believing that other people will compensate and pick up the slack.

It therefore seems that other people can help us work harder and improve our performance if a) they are also working hard and b) we know our own performance is being tracked.

CLASSROOM IMPLICATIONS

Other research has emerged that suggests that, when given the choice, people will choose environments that do not require them to put in high levels of effort. Our default setting seems to be one of preserving energy, not expending it.

This has some interesting implications for where children sit in the classroom. This means not letting students always choose who they sit next to, but instead pairing students with someone who will encourage them to work hard (#44). The person they like the most may not be the person who helps them work at their best. The authors of this study, from universities in Hamburg and Brussels, succinctly summarise their findings by stating that "simply performing a task next to a person who exerts a lot of effort in a task will help you do the same".

THE ONE ABOUT TEACHER EVALUATION

@inner_drive | www.innerdrive.co.uk

THE STUDY

Does student evaluation of a teacher bear any relation to how good that teacher actually is? Most students will have a favourite teacher, but is this based on who they like the most rather than who helps them learn the most? This would mean that student ratings of teacher effectiveness were more akin to a popularity contest than anything else.

Eager to answer this question, researchers ran a thorough review of the existing studies in this area. As well as re-analysing previously reported reviews, they also added the most up-to-date studies in their evaluation.

THE MAIN FINDINGS

1 There was **no correlation between how much students rated the effectiveness of their teacher** and how much they actually learned. The authors of the study could not be clearer when they stated that "despite more than 75 years of sustained effort, there is presently no evidence supporting the widespread belief that students learn more from professors who receive higher student evaluation ratings".

2 **Previous studies that had found a positive link between the two** were likely suffering from the result of having a very small sample size (which can make the studies less reliable) or from a publication bias, which is where researchers are more likely to publish positive findings rather than negative ones.

3 It is **complex and difficult to measure** how much someone has learnt. So much so that "the entire notion that we could measure professors' teaching effectiveness by simple ways such as asking students to answer a few questions about their perceptions of their course experiences, instructor knowledge, and the like seems unrealistic".

Ref: Uttl et al, 2017, *Studies in Educational Evaluation*

THE ONE ABOUT TEACHER EVALUATION

RELATED RESEARCH

Other research has explored why some students rate their teachers as more effective than others. Two main factors might be at play here. The first is that one of the strongest predictors of how students rate their teacher is the level of prior interest that those students had in the subject. Simply put: if we like a topic a lot then we are more likely to rate the person teaching that topic as very good. The reverse is also true, as most students don't tend to like the person who makes them work hard at the subject they don't like.

The second factor around student evaluation may be a sense of confirmation bias. In previous studies, students received a brief biography of a supply teacher which were identical except for one detail. Half the students read that this teacher was "warm", and the other half read that they had a "cold" personality. At the end of the lesson, students who had been primed to think of their new teacher as warm were more likely to rate them as such, whereas those who had been conditioned to think of them as cold were more likely to rate them as being distant and aloof. It seems that teachers' reputations often precede them, strongly influencing how the new cohort think and feel about them.

CLASSROOM IMPLICATIONS

The authors of this study, from Mount Royal University in Canada, state that universities and colleges focused on student learning may need to give minimal or no weight to student evaluation ratings. That is not to say that the student voice is not important. How students feel towards their studies and the beliefs they have about those teaching must be heard; they just shouldn't be important criteria for measuring how effective their teachers are.

If educational institutions really want to know how effective their teachers are, they may do well to consider teacher levels of grit and optimism, as some research suggests that this may be a better predictor (#75).

THE ONE ABOUT TALENT BIAS

@inner_drive | www.innerdrive.co.uk

THE STUDY

What are we more in awe of: natural ability or hard work? A lot of people in education and sport claim to really value the importance of persistence and resilience, but are we all secretly holding a "natural talent bias"?

Researchers ran a study in which they played two pieces of music to a range of musicians. The first, they were told, was described as "a natural" who had early evidence of innate ability. The second was labelled as a "striver" as they had demonstrated high levels of motivation and determination.

In reality, both pieces of music were from the same professional musician. The participants in the study then had to rate which sounded better and which would go on to have a better career.

THE MAIN FINDINGS

1 Despite hearing music from the same musician, the participants in the study **rated the "natural"** as more talented, more likely to be successful and the better choice to join their orchestra **than the "striver"**.

2 At the start of the experiment, the participants had stated that hard work and training were essential for a musician to succeed. This view was endorsed more by the expert musicians. However, the expert musicians **were found to be more impressed** by the "natural" musician than their less experienced counterparts.

3 When given the choice of who they would like to hear play again, the **experts went for the "natural"** and rated their ability higher.

Ref: Tsay and Banaji, 2011, *Journal of Experimental Social Psychology*

THE ONE ABOUT TALENT BIAS

RELATED RESEARCH

A similar cognitive bias to the "natural talent effect" is the "halo effect". This is where people are influenced by someone's initial positive performance when they come to assess their second piece of work. One such study found that teachers who graded a student's first piece assignment highly were more likely to give them a better grade on their second unrelated piece of work.

Research suggests that one way to avoid this is to anonymise the performer from their performance. Evidence suggests that having blind auditions in music and anonymous CVs for job applications helps to overcome this faulty thinking. It has been suggested that similar measures for student's work may help mitigate this in schools. However, it should be noted that this would in itself present some challenges when providing feedback based on a student's development and progress.

CLASSROOM IMPLICATIONS

This study, from Harvard University, has interesting implications for how people view talent. As the authors of the study note, "almost as complex as talent itself is the ability to recognize it". If people are seduced by natural talent, then those who show early signs of higher ability may be singled out for increased or special attention. This is problematic, especially when you consider a recent piece of research showing that how well a child does at primary school is closely related to the month in which they are born. This means that children at primary school may appear more talented within a year group than they are, because of age-related effects. This effect almost completely disappears by the time students leave high school.

Another issue that this study raises is how subsequently we help people develop their skills. If we say we value hard work and effort but, by our actions, actually value natural ability, then this message is likely to be picked up by our students. If students believe that hard work and effort will make little difference as they will always be behind their more "naturally talented" peers, then will this not mean that they are less likely to put in hard work and demonstrate resilience?

THE ONE ABOUT RETRIEVAL PRACTICE

@inner_drive | www.innerdrive.co.uk

THE STUDY

Researchers studied the impact of different study strategies on how much students learn. One such strategy is "Retrieval Practice", sometimes referred to as "The Testing Effect", which describes the act of having to come up with an answer to a question.

They tested how effective this strategy was compared to simply reading and re-reading key passages. As well as comparing final test scores, they also measured how effective the students thought these strategies were and how interesting they found their revision sessions whilst doing them.

THE MAIN FINDINGS

1 If the final test was 2–7 days away, students who had **one study period followed by a session of retrieval practice did at least 30% better** than those who had done two study periods of reading.

2 The longer you need to remember information, the **more powerful** "The Testing Effect" is.

3 The longer you need to remember information for, the **less effective** reading is.

Final Exam Performance

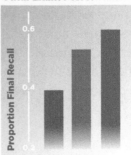

Proportion Final Recall

0.6
0.4
0.2

"Did it Help Me?"

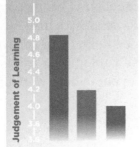

Judgement of Learning

5.0
4.8
4.6
4.4
4.2
4.0
3.8
3.6

■ Reading, Reading, Reading, Reading ■ Reading, Reading, Reading, Testing ■ Reading, Testing, Testing, Testing

4 Students were most likely to rate re-reading as being **more effective** than retrieval practice. However, the students who used mainly retrieval practice **remembered over 50% more** than those who had just read and re-read during revision.

5 Students who had revised using retrieval practice found it **more interesting** than those who had just read the material.

Ref: Roediger and Karpicke, 2006, *Psychological Science*

THE ONE ABOUT RETRIEVAL PRACTICE

RELATED RESEARCH

The benefits of retrieval practice have been studied for more than 100 years. They have been found to be especially strong during stressful situations, such as taking final exams (#76). Other research confirms that providing immediate feedback after testing can further enhance these benefits, and this also helps students identify any potential gaps in their knowledge.

Other research suggests that replicating exam conditions whilst studying for a test further enhances the ability to recall information in their final exam. Essentially, practicing the ability to recall information improves our ability to do so.

The findings from this study - that students incorrectly believe that re-reading is a better strategy compared with retrieval practice - is both interesting and alarming. However, if students are intent on mainly reading whilst studying, other evidence (#34) suggests they should do so out loud and with no background noise (#80).

CLASSROOM IMPLICATIONS

The results from this study, from Washington University, have some important implications for how we can help our students learn key material in preparation for their exams. It suggests that they may be likely to choose ineffective strategies at the expense of more-effective ones unless we help educate them as to the best learning strategies.

The researchers also touch on another important bonus of using retrieval practice regularly when they state that "frequent testing leads students to space their study effort". This backs up existing research that shows that spacing out your learning leads to far greater retention and recall than massed learning (i.e. cramming). Therefore, it seems imperative that we clearly teach students not just about the importance of studying, but how to do so more efficiently and effectively.

The results from this study couldn't be clearer. Studying isn't just something that students do in order to do well in a test. Tests are something students should do in order to study more effectively.

THE ONE ABOUT THOUGHT SUPPRESSION

@inner_drive | www.innerdrive.co.uk

THE STUDY

In one of the most iconic studies in psychology, researchers asked participants to verbalise their thoughts for five minutes into a tape recorder.

They were told to not think about white bears. They were asked to ring the bell in front of them every time they thought of a white bear or said the words "white bear".

THE MAIN FINDINGS

1 Despite trying to **not think about white bears**, participants did so at least once per minute.

2 Participants were **most likely to think** about white bears when they reached the end of a sentence or in moments of silence.

3 Trying to not think about something makes someone **more likely to think** about that thing. This is known as **"The Rebound Effect"**. This is because people have a preoccupation with the thought they are trying to suppress.

4 Participants who were told to **focus on a red car** instead of trying to suppress thoughts of a white bear **fared better**.

They still struggled to not think of white bears, but **had less of a rebound effect** than those who simply thought "don't think of a white bear".

Ref: Wegner et al, 1987, *Journal of Personality and Social Psychology*

THE ONE ABOUT THOUGHT SUPPRESSION

 ## RELATED RESEARCH

The notion that people have unwanted thoughts that they want to stop dates back to Sigmund Freud's work in the late 19th century. Since then, further research has suggested that our ability to disregard thoughts and information is not very good. For example, studies have shown that juries are influenced by information that the judge has told them to ignore. Likewise, other research suggests that people who try to suppress emotionally difficult events are more likely to suffer later in life from negative psychological and physiological consequences.

As well as the thought distraction technique used in this study, other studies have found that saying the word "stop" is effective at halting a train of thought. This has helped people manage frustration, overcome nerves, sleep better and stop dwelling on worst-case scenarios. People may not be able to control the first thing that pops into their head, but they can control subsequent thoughts and actions.

CLASSROOM IMPLICATIONS

Results from this study, from Trinity University and The University of Texas, show the difficulties, if not impossibilities, of trying to not think about things. As the authors note, "to suppress a thought requires that one a) plans to suppress a thought and b) carry out that plan by suppressing all manifestations of the thought, including the original plan". Yet many of our students try this sort of strategy when it comes to preparing for pressurised moments, such as public speaking or exams. These include saying to themselves "don't rush", "don't mumble your words", "don't misread the question" and "don't say something dumb". Thinking like this paradoxically makes those things more likely to occur.

This study concludes by stating that "suppression is difficult because thinking without focus is difficult". Indeed, attempted thought suppression often leads to a preoccupation and, indeed, a rumination of the thoughts that people had wanted to avoid. This study suggests that it would be better to focus on what you want to achieve, not on what you want to avoid. This includes phrases such as "take my time", "speak clearly", "read the question twice" and "think about what I want to say". The implication is clear: don't think "don't".

THE ONE ABOUT EFFECTIVE FEEDBACK

@inner_drive | www.innerdrive.co.uk

THE STUDY

What constitutes good feedback? Is feedback always helpful? And most importantly, how can teachers give it better? Researchers were keen to answer these questions and so conducted a comprehensive and thorough review of a wide range of studies examining the impact of feedback. Their results make for some very interesting and, in places, quite surprising reading.

THE MAIN FINDINGS

1 Feedback interventions, on average, **significantly improve** student performance. Therefore, if delivered correctly, they can really help students improve their learning.

2 They found that feedback to students can also be detrimental, with over one third of feedback interventions **doing more harm than good**. Essentially, these students would have **done better** if they had been left alone rather than been given feedback.

3 The more that feedback is about the person's ability, the **more likely it was to hinder** their future efforts. At the other end of the spectrum, if the feedback focused on how to do the task better, it was **much more likely to enhance performance**.

4 Feedback that focuses on improving motivation is also **likely to improve subsequent efforts**. However, if students become reliant on this motivational feedback, then when it is withdrawn it **can lead to** a decline in performance.

Ref: Kluger and DeNisi, 1996, *Psychological Bulletin*

THE ONE ABOUT EFFECTIVE FEEDBACK

RELATED RESEARCH

The finding in this study that feedback regarding a person's ability often leads to a decrease in performance is consistent with other existing research (#52). For example, praising someone's ability has been found to lead to a fixed mindset, whereas praising their efforts has been found to enhance intrinsic motivation (#5, #16).

Other research into feedback has found that comparing students to one another, or over-praising them, can lead to an increase in narcissistic behaviour (#65). Also, giving feedback and praise excessively can often convey a low sense of expectation. As a result, this can be demotivating.

As well as considering the type of feedback to give students (#97), research about when to give feedback has given some interesting results. In studies based in a laboratory, delayed feedback was found to be helpful. However, in studies based in real-world environments, immediate feedback has generally been found to be more beneficial. This is probably because when the task is simple or plenty of time is available, delayed feedback helps, whilst if things are left for too long then people forget things or their memories of the event become distorted.

CLASSROOM IMPLICATIONS

This study has some important implications for classroom feedback. As the authors of the study comment, "feedback interventions are double edge swords because feedback interventions do not always increase performance and under certain conditions are detrimental to performance". This suggests that teachers should not always rush to give feedback, as more is not always better. If feedback is given at the wrong time or is the wrong type of feedback, it will likely hinder instead of help.

The challenge that teachers face is that sometimes their managers want them to give more feedback to students and that students regularly report that they like receiving feedback. The authors of the study could not be clearer when they warn that "practitioners confuse their feelings that feedback is desirable with the question of whether feedback interventions benefit performance". Seeing feedback in terms of quality and not of quantity will help teachers reduce workload whilst simultaneously improving student learning.

THE ONE ABOUT MOTIVATING BORED STUDENTS

@inner_drive | www.innerdrive.co.uk

THE STUDY

Students were divided into two groups before they had to watch a boring lecture. To replicate the complaint of "boring lessons", the lecture was presented in a dull fashion, in a monotonous style and without any enhancing embellishments.

Prior to the lecture, the study group of students were briefly told why and how this lecture would help them in the future. It was acknowledged that the lecture might not be fun, but they were encouraged to persist. The second group, which was the control group, did not receive any message before the class.

THE MAIN FINDINGS

The impact on the study group of hearing the brief rationale of the lesson beforehand compared to the control group was:

1 **Enhanced motivation** during the lesson.

2 Higher levels of engagement during the lesson. This **effect increased as the lesson went on**, with a **25%** difference between them and the control group by the end.

3 Significantly **more interest in the subject** that they were being taught; they also rated it as more important to them.

.

4 Increased rate of learning, demonstrating **up to** **11%** **higher levels of both factual and conceptual knowledge** of the topic after the lecture.

Ref: Jang, 2008, *Journal of Educational Psychology*

THE ONE ABOUT MOTIVATING BORED STUDENTS

RELATED RESEARCH

Previously, researchers had investigated how best to help encourage people when faced with a boring task (and therefore when intrinsic and internal motivation are lacking). One such experiment had subjects press a button on a keyboard every time a light was flashed. To help combat this boring task, they found that giving a rationale of the task, acknowledging the learner's perspective (i.e. the negative feelings they may be experiencing) and talking to them in a non-controlling way that emphasised choice instead of pressure significantly boosted performance.

Other studies have found that, when students do not value what they have been asked to learn, both their motivation and engagement levels dip (#47). This becomes increasingly evident and important as students get older, when independent learning becomes an essential component of academic success.

However, other research has emphasised the importance of the role of the teacher-student relationship in motivating students (#83). It may not be just about what you say but how you say it that also matters. The research suggests factors such as perceived warmth, trust and relatedness are important.

CLASSROOM IMPLICATIONS

This research suggests that, in a quest to motivate students, we need to highlight how learning the topic will benefit them and remind them that they have the personal capacity to overcome the challenges of learning it. As the researcher of the study, from the University of Wisconsin, concludes, "to facilitate student's motivation, rationales need to produce two effects: students need to see the importance and personal utility within the task, and students need to perceive high autonomy while working on that task".

Many educators are encouraged to share the learning outcomes of their lesson with the students at the start. However, this may not be enough to motivate them to learn. In this study, the researcher not only explained the learning outcomes, but also highlighted four key areas: why it would help, how it would help, acknowledgement that it would be difficult and encouragement for the students to be persistent. This can be done quickly at the start of a lesson and, for little extra effort, promises large rewards.

THE ONE ABOUT SELF-ANALYSIS OVER TIME

@inner_drive | www.innerdrive.co.uk

THE STUDY

Researchers examined if people downgrade their assessment of their past selves in order to inflate their feelings about their current achievements. Their study, entitled "From Chump to Champ: People's Appraisals of Their Earlier and Present Selves", makes for fascinating reading.

THE MAIN FINDINGS

1 Peoples' descriptions of their present selves were **more favourable** than their portrayals of their past selves.

2 This finding, of **criticising our past self** as a way of praising our current self, was **consistent amongst both students and adults**.

3 The **longer the gap** between their past self and current self, **the more likely** they were to criticise their past self.

4 Participants believed that their **current self was better** than their past self, even if no actual improvement had taken place.

5 People were likely to believe that they had **improved their personality traits**. However, this belief did not extend to their acquaintances, with participants more likely to state that other people had **remained the same**.

6 The **more important the skill was** to someone, the more likely they were **to believe** that they had improved it over time.

Ref: Wilson and Ross, 2001, *Journal of Personality and Social Psychology*

THE ONE ABOUT SELF-ANALYSIS OVER TIME

 ## RELATED RESEARCH

The results from this study supports previous research which found that people are more likely to rate themselves as being happier now than they were in the past. Indeed, people have a very odd perception of time, with things that happened at either the start or at the end of an event weighing heavily in our minds (#98).

Other research suggests that the more motivated we are to feel good about ourselves, the more likely we are to praise our current self at the expense of our past self. This helps boost our current self-worth and insulates us from doubt, worry and nerves.

A wealth of research has found that most people rate their skills and personality as above average. Indeed, in Western cultures people are often encouraged to think highly of themselves. However, by criticising their past self, people are able to boost how they feel now without having to actually get better or confront the reality of remaining the same in the face of current evidence. This is similar to the Dunning-Kruger effect, which states that having low ability often leads to an inflated sense of one's current ability (#18).

CLASSROOM IMPLICATIONS

Being able to accurately assess one's current level of ability is a fundamental part of learning. It provides the platform from which all learning stems. If our students believe they are progressing based only on an overly negative view of the past, then this can hinder their motivation to actually get better. As the authors of the study note, "by evaluating former identities less favourably than current ones, individuals can judge themselves to be improving".

They also go on to state that "just as advertisers creatively manipulate evidence to showcase constantly 'new and improved' products, so too might individuals repackage and revise themselves to highlight improvement on important dimensions". This may provide a short-term boost to their confidence. Unfortunately, this type of confidence is not very robust or durable. The best way to help students feel confident is to increase their competence through raising their knowledge and skills.

THE ONE ABOUT ASKING WHY

@inner_drive | www.innerdrive.co.uk

THE STUDY

If we want students to remember key facts, should we a) simply tell them the information, b) tell them the information plus an explanation of why it is true or c) tell them the information and have them think about why this might be the case?

In order to answer this question, researchers placed students in one of three groups. Some read a list of sentences, such as "the hungry man got in his car". Others read these sentences along with an explanation afterwards (i.e. "the hungry man got in his car to go to the restaurant"). Finally, the rest of the students read the sentences and then had to answer a question: "why would he do that?".

THE MAIN FINDINGS

Students who had **just read the list of sentences** recalled, on average,

37% of them correctly.

Those who had the **sentence and an explanation** recalled

35% of them correctly.

However, those who had **seen the sentence** and had had to come up with **their own explanation** (i.e. asking **"why would he do that?"**) were able to recall an impressive

71% of the sentences.

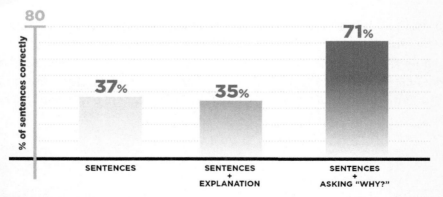

Ref: Pressley et al, 1987, *Journal of Experimental Psychology*

THE ONE ABOUT ASKING WHY

RELATED RESEARCH

A growing body of research has found that the more students have to think and process information themselves the more likely they are to remember it. This is why students who had to generate their own answers by asking themselves "why would that be the case" outperformed those who had been given the explanation. Psychologists have labelled this technique "elaborative interrogation". A recent and very comprehensive review found that this is one of the most effective strategies students can utilise to boost their memory.

Additional research has examined other reasons why asking, "why would this be the case?" or "why is this true for X but not for Y?" may help. Possible explanations include that it arouses a sense of curiosity and that it helps link the new information to pre-existing knowledge. This, in turn, ingrains the new information into the long-term memory.

CLASSROOM IMPLICATIONS

This technique of asking yourself "why?" may be better suited to some students rather than others. For example, the authors of this study, from the University of Notre Dame, the University of Minnesota and the University of Western Ontario, note that "novices, lacking topical knowledge, often do not automatically link newly encountered relations to information that could make the significance of the relations more understandable and thus, make the material more memorable".

This suggests that elaborative interrogation may be particularly effective for students who already have a wide breadth and depth of knowledge or as a final study technique once a lot of the learning has already occurred. It would also be advisable for students to use this technique in the presence of a teacher, so that the answers they generate are checked for accuracy. This will avoid having to repeat and memorise inaccurate information.

THE ONE ABOUT SLEEP

@inner_drive | www.innerdrive.co.uk

THE STUDY

We all do it. Only a few of us are getting enough of it and most of us want a bit more. On average we spend over 20 years of our life doing it, but the benefits of sleeping are still underappreciated. Despite The National Sleep Foundation recommending that teenagers need up to ten hours a night, many report getting less than seven.

Researchers reviewed the many different functions that sleep plays and how important it is in terms of students' memory, emotional regulation and mood. Their findings confirm that it is a fundamental part of the thinking and learning processes.

THE MAIN FINDINGS

1 Having **a good night's sleep** prior to learning allows students to create **new memory associations more effectively**. This is known as their ability to "encode information".

2 If students do not get **enough sleep**, it **hinders their ability** to commit what they have been taught to memory. This is known as an inability to "consolidate information".

3 When **sleep-deprived**, people are more likely to forget positive memories. The opposite is true with negative memories, with tired students being more likely to retain and recall these.

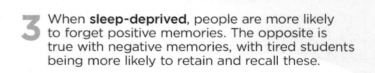

4 **Excessive sleep loss** increases the likelihood of students displaying negative emotions, feeling stressed and being unable to manage their emotions.

Ref: Walker and van der Helm, 2009, *Psychological Bulletin*

THE ONE ABOUT SLEEP

RELATED RESEARCH

This review confirms the findings of other sleep research. As well as sleep being linked to memory, mood and emotional control, evidence suggests that there is a strong relationship between quality and quantity of sleep and our ability to concentrate. This may be part of why the amount of sleep students get has been found to correlate with the grades they achieve. Yet, despite the importance of sleep, parents often don't know how much sleep their child is getting (#92).

Other research has found a link between getting a good night's sleep and creativity and insightfulness, with participants twice as likely to find out the hidden rule to completing a puzzle if they had slept well the night before. Separate research has also found that teenagers who don't get enough sleep or who have irregular sleep patterns are more likely to fall ill, as sleep washes away toxins that have built up during the day.

CLASSROOM IMPLICATIONS

The need to educate students about the importance of sleep is paramount, as many may be unaware of just how important it is. The authors of this study, from the University of California, conclude their paper by stating "when troubled, get to bed, you'll feel better in the morning". It appears that by doing so they will also be more likely to recall what they have been taught previously and be more receptive to learning more in the future.

As well as teaching how important sleep is, we also need to tell students about some common sleep mistakes. These include going to bed at different times each night (as this confuses the body's internal body clock) and having excessively long naps earlier in the day. Other sleep mistakes include watching TV and being on mobile phones right before bed.

Mobile phone usage late at night is particularly prevalent, with one study linking late-night texting or calling to declines in mood, self-esteem and coping ability. It is worth considering involving parents in this discussion as well. This will help, as evidence suggests that the teenage brain struggles with self-control more than the adult brain, meaning that teens may benefit from others initially making that decision for them.

THE ONE ABOUT MOBILE PHONES

@inner_drive | www.innerdrive.co.uk

THE STUDY

Mobile phones are a part of everyday life. They have the power to connect people and can be great tools for learning. Most people have their mobile phone next to them for large parts of the day. But is there a darker side to mobile phones? Can the mere presence of a mobile phone negatively affect student performance?

To answer this question, researchers had students complete a concentration task with either a mobile phone or a notepad on the table near them. The students didn't use the phone during the experiment, it was just within their eye-line.

To gather further information, the researchers had students complete a range of questionnaires about themselves and also ran the experiment twice; once with someone else's phone near them and once with their own phone.

THE MAIN FINDINGS

1 The mere presence of a mobile phone led to a **20%** **reduction in attention, concentration and performance** in tasks that were demanding and complex (i.e. ones that students had to think hard about).

2 Students **performed worse** in these tasks, regardless of whether they could see their own **phone nearby** or someone else's.

3 This **reduction in performance was found to be true** regardless of the student's gender, age, how much they normally used their own phone or how attached they said they felt to it.

Ref: Thornton et al, 2014, *Social Psychology*

THE ONE ABOUT MOBILE PHONES

RELATED RESEARCH

The numerous and wide-ranging costs of excessive mobile phone use have been well documented in psychological research. For example, research has linked students who are on their phone in class to worse grades, and those that do so excessively report higher levels of stress, anxiety and a fear of missing out. Frequency of students using their phone for social networking and texting is also negatively correlated to their grades.

A lot of research has been conducted on the impact of using a phone late at night, with people who do so for longer than 20 minutes at a time reporting getting less sleep each night, and their sleep is of a lower quality. Other research (#90) has also found a link between all screen time (i.e. phones, TV, tablets, computers) and a reduction in well-being, diet quality and concentration.

CLASSROOM IMPLICATIONS

A recent survey found that 81% of people report never turning their phone off. Therefore, having it on and nearby, even if it is not being used, is a common aspect of daily student life. But at what cost? Students suffer from a drop in concentration when the phone is nearby, but as the authors of this study note, "the distracting effect of the cell phone's mere presence was not observed on the simple tasks, but was more apparent on complex tasks".

Why might this be the case? The authors of this study, from the University of Southern Maine, conclude by suggesting that "it is easier to maintain task attention when there are fewer stimuli present that may evoke thoughts unrelated to the task". Perhaps this could be one reason why a recent review found that schools who banned mobile phones saw an increase in student grades. This effect was observed most in struggling students (#49).

Given that learning can be cognitively demanding, it is fair to assume that students should not be studying in sight of their phones. Out of sight really does seem to be out of mind.

THE ONE ABOUT MARSHMALLOWS, RELIABILITY AND SELF-CONTROL

@inner_drive | www.innerdrive.co.uk

THE STUDY

The famous "Marshmallow Test" found that students who can delay gratification (i.e. work hard now on the promise of future rewards) do better at school and in life. In this test, researchers offered children one marshmallow. The children were told by the researcher that they could either eat it straight away or wait and be rewarded with two marshmallows later. The time the children held off eating the first marshmallow was used as a measure of delayed gratification.

But what if the students don't trust their teacher? Researchers divided students into two groups. Before giving them the choice of eating a marshmallow right away or waiting for another one, they had the students either see the teacher break a promise (and therefore appear unreliable) or keep a promise (i.e. be seen to be reliable). They then measured how long the different students waited before they ate the first marshmallow.

THE MAIN FINDINGS

1 Children who thought the **teacher was unreliable** waited for an average of around **3 minutes** before eating the marshmallow.

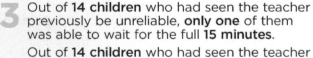

2 Children who thought that the **teacher was reliable** waited for an average of over **12 minutes** before eating the marshmallow.

3 Out of **14 children** who had seen the teacher previously be unreliable, **only one** of them was able to wait for the full **15 minutes**.

Out of **14 children** who had seen the teacher previously keep their word, **nine** of them were able to wait the full **15 minutes**.

4 The impact of **seeing someone either lie or keep their word** impacted all students' ability to delay gratification. This was true regardless of age and gender.

Ref: Kidd et al, 2013, *Cognition*

THE ONE ABOUT MARSHMALLOWS, RELIABILITY AND SELF-CONTROL

 ## RELATED RESEARCH

This study advances our understanding of delayed gratification. Before this experiment, studies had predominantly put the emphasis on an individual's capacity to wait (#13). In fact, in studies that did not account for teacher reliability as a factor, the average wait time before succumbing to the marshmallow temptation was around six minutes. This is half the wait time of the reliable teacher condition and twice as long as the unreliable teacher condition in this experiment.

Other research has found that young children are particularly sensitive to uncertainty about their future. It therefore stands to reason that if children are not convinced that they will receive a later reward for delaying the gratification, then there is no reason to do so. As the authors of the study note, "waiting is only the rational choice if you believe that a second marshmallow is likely to actually appear after a reasonably short delay – and that the marshmallow is not at risk of being taken away".

CLASSROOM IMPLICATIONS

The authors of the study conclude by saying that "we demonstrated that children's sustained decisions to wait for a greater reward rather than quickly taking a lesser reward are strongly influenced by the reliability of the environment (in this case, the reliability of the researcher's verbal assurances)". If reliability is a significant mediator or children's ability to delay gratification, consideration must be given as to what teachers can do to help develop trust with their students and facilitate a consistent and stable environment (#81).

Strategies include consistency and clarity. If students have a clear understanding of what is expected of them, what the rules are and what the consequences will be, then ambiguity and doubt will be reduced. Likewise, consistently and regularly enforcing these rules will help ensure reliability. They may not always agree with what you say, or always like what you do, but they will trust you more.

THE ONE ABOUT NOTE-TAKING

@inner_drive | www.innerdrive.co.uk

THE STUDY

Have you ever wondered if students should take notes during class or fully focus on what the teacher is saying? Does the learner's previous experience with the material make a difference? Are some notes better for different types of learning than others? Research conducted at the University of California over 30 years ago has already comprehensively answered all these questions.

THE MAIN FINDINGS

Notes vs no notes

1 Students who **took notes** during a lesson performed **12% better** on a problem-solving test afterwards compared to those who took no notes at all.

2 However, students who **took no notes** did marginally better on questions that required them to recall **facts, stats and quotes** that were said.

The type of notes

3 In a follow-up study, students who **took summary notes** at either the end of the lecture or the end of each topic did **10–15% better** on problem-solving questions and **13–17% better** on recalling facts than those who just took notes during the lesson.

Who benefits most from note-taking

4 Taking summary notes was found to benefit both students who were already familiar with the topic, as well as those who were new to it.

Ref: Peper and Mayer, 1986, *Journal of Educational Psychology*

THE ONE ABOUT NOTE-TAKING

RELATED RESEARCH

These results support a lot of the existing research into note-taking, with evidence suggesting that taking too many notes can be distracting and overload the working memory. This is perhaps why students who took summary notes instead of constant notes throughout the lesson performed better.

It is now commonplace for many students to take notes on their laptops instead of using pen and paper. However, a recent study (#72) has found that students who did so on laptops were more likely to transcribe the lesson word for word without reflecting on it. Those who had taken notes with a pen and paper were more likely to selectively write down key parts and to paraphrase it into their own words. This might play a key role in strengthening memories.

The other advantage of taking notes in your own words is that it increases the chances of making an emotional connection to the content. Research has shown that the more emotionally powerful a memory is, the more likely it is to be stored in long-term memory.

CLASSROOM IMPLICATIONS

Taking notes can be a double-edged sword. If done correctly, they can help students pay attention during the lesson and block out distractions. They also give them a record of what has been said, which students can later refer back to. As well as this, as the researchers of the study point out, "note-taking can encourage the learner to actively build external connections between what is presented and what he or she already knows".

However, if done incorrectly, there can be a cost. Excessive note-taking can take up valuable processing time, which takes focus away from what the teacher is saying. This leaves students constantly playing catch up. Writing down everything verbatim in real time does not leave enough time for students to think about, consider and relate what is being said to their existing knowledge and experiences.

A combination of some summary notes to help improve focus and keep a record of what has been said, whilst emphasising the importance of fully listening to the teacher and reflecting on what they are saying, offers the most sensible strategy.

THE ONE ABOUT IMPOSTOR SYNDROME

@inner_drive | www.innerdrive.co.uk

THE STUDY

Impostor Syndrome describes the belief that you are not as talented as others believe, that your success is down to luck and that one day soon your lack of ability is going to be exposed in front of everyone. Interestingly, it is often experienced by high-achieving individuals.

Initially, this was researched by a pair of psychologists who felt like frauds themselves. They wanted to explore the characteristics of Impostor Syndrome and what, if anything, can be done to help manage and overcome it.

THE MAIN FINDINGS

1 **Impostor Syndrome** was associated with:

Neuroticism
Increased fear and worry

Perfectionism
Unrealistic or unobtainable goals

Low self-efficacy
Doubt their abilities

2 People who suffer from Impostor Syndrome are **more likely** to rate themselves in a **consistently negative manner** across most situations.

3 **20%** of people were found to suffer from Impostor Syndrome, with it affecting **both men and women** pretty much equally.

4 **Social support** can play a high role in mitigating the effects of Impostor Syndrome.

Ref: Vergauwe et al, 2015, *Journal of Business and Psychology*

THE ONE ABOUT IMPOSTOR SYNDROME

RELATED RESEARCH

Impostor Syndrome has been found to be associated with depression and a decline in mental health. Interestingly, other research has found the prevalence of Impostor Syndrome is even higher than reported in this study, with one journal reporting that 43% of students in the study had Impostor Syndrome tendencies.

The fact that this study found that both men and women equally experience Impostor Syndrome is interesting, as it contradicts previous research which had found the syndrome to be more common in females, with high-achieving women most likely to experience it. Indeed, a recent survey found that female students were less likely to describe themselves as "brave" compared to their male peers, with another study finding that young women feel less confident about entering the workplace.

Other research has focused on the developmental factors that contribute towards Impostor Syndrome. These have been found to include family conflict, perceived excessive parental control, an unhealthy and confusing message about the importance of high grades and a high fear of failure.

CLASSROOM IMPLICATIONS

So, what can teachers do to help? The authors of the study state that "despite the accumulation of objective evidence suggesting the contrary, such as remarkable academic achievements and a successful career history, these persons are unable to internalize and accept successful experiences". The key, therefore, is to spend time helping students identify what they did that contributed to their successes and help them to learn how to enjoy the fruits of their labour. Another strategy, as detailed in the study, is to ensure that students can identify and use the social support around them.

Constant feelings of being an impostor may result in students not putting themselves forward in situations that make them nervous, such as auditioning for the school play or trials for sports teams. Helping students to have the courage of their convictions and to step out of their comfort zones are life skills that will benefit them for many years after they have left school.

THE ONE ABOUT READING OUT LOUD

@inner_drive | www.innerdrive.co.uk

THE STUDY

Dr. Seuss once commented that "the more that you read, the more things you will know. The more that you learn, the more places you'll go". But is there a way to read better that means that you are more likely to remember things?

Researchers ran a study where they had students study a list of words in four different ways. These were reading out loud, reading in silence, hearing a recording of themselves and hearing a recording of someone else say the words.

THE MAIN FINDINGS

1 The researchers found that the study conditions that were most effective through to least effective were:

▶ **Studying by reading the words out loud**

▶ **Studying by hearing a recording of yourself**

▶ **Studying by hearing someone else speak to you**

▶ **Studying by reading in silence**

2 The gap between reading aloud and hearing a recording of themselves was quite small, with only **3%** difference in the final exam separating them.

3 The biggest gap was between the studying by reading the words out loud and reading them in silence, with the former performing **12%** better than the latter.

Ref: Forrin and MacLeod, 2018, *Memory*

THE ONE ABOUT READING OUT LOUD

 ## RELATED RESEARCH

The increase in learning caused by reading out loud is an example of the Production Effect. The Production Effect is caused by producing something with the new information right away in order to anchor it in your mind, rather than it drifting away because of other distractions. This is why drawing whilst learning helps, as it produces a new picture (#82).

Reading out loud does this by utilising a combination of three processes: it is an active event (i.e. you are not passive during the event), it requires an element of visual processing (i.e. seeing the words) and is self-referential (i.e. "*I* said it").

These results also confirm previous findings from research (#70) that suggest that, when students learn information using a combination and variety of senses, it leads to an increase in learning. This is because a multi-pronged approach provides a range of connections in the student's brain, ensuring that the material is more likely to be ingrained in the long-term memory (#41).

CLASSROOM IMPLICATIONS

Given that that many students often choose and prefer to read their notes as part of their revision, the results from this study are very important as they show that some methods of revising by reading are better than others. Teaching students about the importance of reading out loud instead of in silence could help aid them by improving their rate of learning and, indeed, their performance in exams.

The authors conclude by stating that studying and rehearsal "is so valuable in learning and remembering [as] we do it ourselves and we do it in our own voices. When it comes time to recover the information, we can use this distinctive component to help us to remember".

However, a word of caution is needed. Although reading aloud was found to be the most effective of the options available in this study, other research has shown that simply reading the material is a lot less effective than other strategies, such as retrieval practice (#23). Therefore, relying only on reading one's notes during study sessions, even if it is done aloud, may not be the most effective way to learn the material.

THE ONE ABOUT EATING BREAKFAST

@inner_drive | www.innerdrive.co.uk

THE STUDY

Many students report skipping eating breakfast on a regular basis. But is there a cost to this?

To find out, researchers ran a study that compared students who ate breakfast, drank a glucose drink instead, or skipped breakfast altogether. As well as administering concentration tests throughout the morning, the researchers also ran a memory recall exam and had the students report how they were feeling.

THE MAIN FINDINGS

Concentration levels

1 All students had **a dip in their ability to focus** as the morning went on. However, if students had **eaten breakfast**, this decline was **reduced by 50–65%** compared to those who hadn't.

2 For the first few hours, **having a glucose drink** instead of skipping breakfast actually led to a **bigger drop** in student's attention levels.

Memory recall

3 In a memory test conducted four hours after a revision session, students who had **not had breakfast** suffered **12%** reduction in their score. Students who had **only had a glucose drink** for breakfast had a **27%** decline, with those who **had breakfast improving** their performance by **3–5%**.

Alertness

4 Students who ate breakfast felt the **most alert over the course of the morning**. A glucose drink gave an initial boost for the first few hours before dropping to the same low levels by mid-day as those who had missed breakfast.

Ref: Wesnes et al, 2003, *Appetite*

THE ONE ABOUT EATING BREAKFAST

 ## RELATED RESEARCH

As well as the benefits to memory and attention demonstrated in this study, there is a wealth of research about the far-reaching benefits of eating breakfast. For example, eating breakfast has been linked to better eating habits throughout the day and improvement to both physical and mental health, as well as boosting energy levels.

Authors of a different study found that "individuals who consumed a cereal breakfast each day were less depressed, less emotionally distressed and had lower levels of perceived stress than those who did not eat breakfast each day". Why might this be the case? Authors of a different review found that "missing meals, especially breakfast, leads to low blood sugar and this causes low mood, irritability and fatigue". It seems that missing breakfast isn't just associated with poorer mental health, it actually causes it. Similar results have also been found for students who miss eating dinner with their parents (#71).

Finally, eating breakfast is associated with better physical activity. In a separate study on school students, both boys and girls who sometimes ate breakfast were found to do less physical activity than those who always did. This is one of the reasons why those who skip breakfast are more likely to become obese and have higher levels of cholesterol.

CLASSROOM IMPLICATIONS

Educating students about the importance of eating breakfast is important. Left to their own devices, many will be tempted to miss it or have a glucose drink substitute. Doing so can have serious consequences for their academic performance. For example, a different study found that the odds of an 11-year-old achieving an above-average score on a test were twice as high for those who ate breakfast compared with those who did not.

In some cases, schools may provide breakfast for some or all their students. As the authors of the study note, "this study provides clear evidence that cereal breakfast has a positive effect on the cognitive function of school children, particularly towards the end of the morning".

THE ONE ABOUT STREAMING

@inner_drive | www.innerdrive.co.uk

THE STUDY

A significant amount of schools group their students by their ability. This is called "streaming". But what impact does this have on students placed in the top, middle and bottom streams? Drawing on a sample size of 19,000 children across the UK and tracking them for five years, researchers investigated the effects.

THE MAIN FINDINGS

1 Compared with those **who were not streamed**, students **who were in the middle** stream performed worse in ...

2 Compared to those **who were not streamed**, students **who were in the bottom** stream performed worse in ...

This effect was most pronounced in maths.

3 Compared to those **who were not streamed**, students **who were in the top** stream performed better in ...

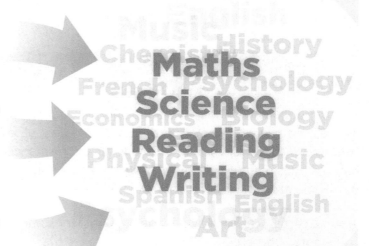

Maths
Science
Reading
Writing

Streaming helps those placed in the top stream, but is significantly worse for those in the middle and bottom streams.

Ref: Parsons and Hallam, 2014, *Oxford Review of Education*

THE ONE ABOUT STREAMING

RELATED RESEARCH

Streaming by ability remains popular in many schools in England. Recent analysis found that it occurs in 19.5% of schools in Wales, 15.6% in England, 15.6% in Scotland and 11.2% in Northern Ireland.

Previously, research has focused on which type of students are most likely to be classified as low ability and therefore to be placed in the bottom stream. This has included variables such as students from lower socio-economic backgrounds, boys, ethnic minorities and those born later in the school year. The latter point is quite interesting, given that those who are the youngest in their school year are more likely to rate themselves as having lower maths, English and overall academic ability (#87).

One study that yielded similar results to this one, tracked the progress of young teenagers in maths and found that being placed in a mixed-ability group was particularly beneficial for low-attaining students, whilst not hindering the performance of higher achieving students. As the authors of this study note, "streaming therefore advantages those who are already high attainers, disadvantaging those who are placed in the middle and lower groups who are deprived of opportunities for working with those who are more advanced" and it "widens the gap between low and high attaining pupils".

CLASSROOM IMPLICATIONS

The role that varying expectations has on performance in relation to different streams has also been examined on three different levels. Firstly, from a student's perspective, being placed in a lower stream can cause a self-fulfilling prophecy, leading to them disengaging and subsequently under-performing. Secondly, teachers who have lower expectations of their students are less likely to ask them challenging questions and to stretch them (#7). This culminates in students being taught different content and entered in lower exams that have a cap on potential grades. As a result, these students will fall even further behind.

Third and finally, parents of students in the bottom stream frequently report having lower aspirations and expectations that their child will stay in education. Therefore, if schools do stream by ability, time and consideration must be spent on ensuring that this doesn't negatively affect parental attitudes towards their child's learning.

THE ONE ABOUT ACADEMIC BUOYANCY

@inner_drive | www.innerdrive.co.uk

THE STUDY

One of the least-known psychological concepts in the area of mindset and motivation is that of academic buoyancy. Whereas resilience tends to refer to a person's ability to overcome large stressful events, academic buoyancy instead focuses on a student's ability to overcome the everyday challenges of school. These challenges include things like doing poorly on a piece of homework or working under the pressure of coursework deadline. As such, it is an important area within educational psychology.

Researchers explored the key components of academic buoyancy and how it can be developed. Their results make for essential reading for those interested in helping students flourish whilst at school.

THE MAIN FINDINGS

The researchers conclude that there are **five components of Academic Buoyancy** that can be targeted to help students overcome the everyday challenges they face at school.

They labelled these components as "The Five Cs"

Confidence
The self-belief that students have that if they work hard then they will have the abilities needed to successfully complete a specific task.

Co-ordination
Better planning, preparation and time management to avoid procrastination.

Commitment
Displaying high levels of resilience, determination and persistence.

Composure
The ability to manage nerves, anxieties and stress.

Control
Focusing on what is important and what they can control.

They also found that **"The Five Cs"** of academic buoyancy **apply to both male and female students**, as well as **younger and older pupils**.

Ref: Martin et al, 2010, *British Journal of Educational Psychology*

THE ONE ABOUT ACADEMIC BUOYANCY

 ## RELATED RESEARCH

Research on academic buoyancy is still in its relative infancy. There is cause to be optimistic, with many of its associated components – such as self-regulation, growth mindset and metacognition – associated with a range of positive outcomes (#61). Resilience, although similar but still distinct from academic buoyancy, has been more heavily researched. Ways to develop resilience have been found to include ensuring high levels of both challenge and support, helpful self-talk and attributing successes to internal factors (#12, #39).

Another interesting area of related research has found that female students have been found to score significantly higher on anxiety scales and report more academic hassles. In terms of age, evidence suggest that the early teenage years are a particularly challenging time with regards to both fluctuating motivation and emotional control.

CLASSROOM IMPLICATIONS

Within their research paper, the authors of the study offer a clear and succinct breakdown of how teachers can help apply their findings in their classroom. They write:

> Developing self-efficacy (confidence) can involve restructuring learning so as to maximise opportunities for success, individualising tasks where possible, addressing and enhancing students' negative beliefs about themselves and developing skills in effective goal setting. Work into self-regulation and goal-setting also provide direction for enhancing students' planning (co-ordination) and persistence (commitment).

With regards to goal setting, encouraging students to set effective goals and showing them how to work towards these goals is an important means of maintaining persistence. Developing students' self-regulatory skills can also be a means of enhancing their capacity to plan and persist in the face of a challenge. This can encompass helping them use their time more effectively; prioritising; being clear about what one is expected or required to do for an assignment, homework and study programmes and developing strategies for checking schoolwork is done.

In terms of control, research suggests that showing students how effort and effective work strategies are key will enhance their sense of control. Control is also developed by providing feedback in effective and consistent ways and providing task-based input on students' work that makes it clear how they can improve.

THE ONE ABOUT THE SPOTLIGHT EFFECT

@inner_drive | www.innerdrive.co.uk

THE STUDY

It has been said that "you'll worry less about what people think about you when you realise how seldom they do". It is easy when under pressure or stressed to believe that all eyes are on you. But are they actually, or is it just a faulty perception in your own head?

The spotlight effect describes the tendency for people to over-estimate how much other people notice their appearance or actions. Keen to study this in students, researchers from Cornell University collaborated in 2000 in a series of quirky and intriguing studies.

THE MAIN FINDINGS

1. In one of their studies, they had participants wear an embarrassing T-shirt to a lecture (the T-shirt of choice was one with Barry Manilow's face on it). The participants predicted that just **under half of their fellow students would notice** the T-shirt. The reality was that **less than a quarter actually did**.

2. The spotlight effect **affected all participants the same**, with no difference between male and female students.

3. The spotlight effect goes beyond just embarrassing situations, with students just as likely to **over-estimate how much people noticed them** when wearing a T-shirt of someone considered cool or iconic (in this case, Martin Luther King Jr, Bob Marley or Jerry Seinfeld).

4. Beyond just appearances, the spotlight effect was found to be **present in social situations** (both positively and negatively). Students thought that other group members would remember both their interesting points as well as their offensive ones more than they actually did.

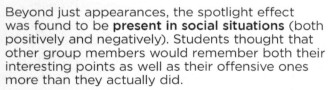

Ref: Gilovich et al, 2000, *Journal of Personality and Social Psychology*

THE ONE ABOUT THE SPOTLIGHT EFFECT

RELATED RESEARCH

Other research has found that we tend to over-emphasise the significance of our own actions. For example, one such study found that people consistently overestimate their own contributions towards a group task. Likewise, other research has found that we tend to assume that our version of reality is objective and not subjective. Finally, people tend to assume that other people will have the same perception as ourselves. These three factors combined can lead to a wide variation in how two people interpret the same event.

The majority of this research has been done with children and is labelled "theory of mind". This describes how some people struggle to understand that others have different beliefs, knowledge and intentions than themselves. This study advances our understanding of this by a) applying it to older students and b) adding a social status element to it.

CLASSROOM IMPLICATIONS

The authors of the study reflected that "people seem to believe that the social spotlight shines more brightly on them than it truly does". What impact does this have? "Individuals do not reach out to others because of a fear of rejection and how it will be perceived; people do not dance, sing, play a musical instrument, or join in the organisation's softball game because of the fear that they will look bad". In a school setting, these examples could easily be students not asking a question in class for fear of looking dumb, not auditioning for the school play through fear of rejection or feeling anxious about public speaking through fear of embarrassing themselves in front of their peers.

The researchers conclude their paper by stating that "the present research suggests that a great many of these fears may be misplaced or exaggerated. Other people may be less likely to notice or remember our shortcomings than we typically expect". Teachers can help students overcome the spotlight by normalising their worries, explaining and demonstrating that everyone suffers from the spotlight effect and creating a culture where mistakes are not met by ridicule and laughter.

THE ONE ABOUT RESILIENCE

@inner_drive | www.innerdrive.co.uk

THE STUDY

There is a growing interest amongst teachers, schools, policy makers and parents in how best to develop resilience in young people. With increasing uncertainty in society and more pressures in the lives of young people, this area is of great importance. But how does one go about developing resilience? What does a research-informed and evidence-based programme look like?

Researchers recently reviewed the existing studies out there to come up with the most comprehensive set of suggestions to date.

THE MAIN FINDINGS

Creating a programme that develops and enhances resilience should focus on three distinct areas, **personal qualities**, a **facilitative environment** and **challenge mindset**.

1 Personal qualities

These include but are not limited to:

- **High personal standards**
- **Optimism**
- **Competitiveness**
- **Intrinsic motivation**
- **Self-confidence**
- **Self-talk**
- **Focusing on what is important and what you can control**

2 A facilitative environment

Ensuring both high levels of challenge and support.

Where resilience happens

	Unrelenting	Facilitative
CHALLENGE	Stagnant	Comfortable

SUPPORT →

3 A challenge mindset

Seeing things as a challenge, not a threat. This can be done by:

- **Focusing on what you stand to gain**
- **Asking yourself "what can I do about this?"**
- **Not catastrophising**
- **Avoiding words like "should and must"**
- **Concentrating on positive and helpful thoughts**

Ref: Fletcher and Sarkar, 2016, *Journal of Sport Psychology in Action*

THE ONE ABOUT RESILIENCE

 ## RELATED RESEARCH

The authors of this study are amongst the leading experts on resilience. Interestingly, some of their work to date has focused on how Olympic gold medalists developed their resilience. They found that athletes who viewed their decisions as active choices and not as sacrifices, as well as who viewed setbacks as opportunities for growth, were more resilient.

Other strategies that these Olympians used included accessing support from those around them, identifying their motivation for succeeding and drawing their confidence from a range of sources (i.e. not just their last results). The same researchers have also investigated resilience in the workplace and have made similar findings.

CLASSROOM IMPLICATIONS

Often with psychological interventions, it is not the "what" but the "how" that matters. Helping others develop resilience needs to be packaged in a way that puts people at ease and is not perceived as either punishment or because they aren't good enough. The authors of the study allude to this, and offer a potential solution, when they write:

> Because misunderstandings exist about resilience, training in this area should begin with an explanation of what resilience is and is not. It should be emphasised that feeling vulnerable to stress or struggling to cope with adversity should not be perceived as weakness. Rather, open discussion about this topic is a sign of strength and the potential beginning of positive change that will hopefully lead to individuals withstanding - and potentially thriving on - pressure.

Once this has been done then "all three areas - personal qualities, facilitative environment and challenge mindset - need to be appropriately addressed to enhance performers' ability to withstand pressure". This three-pronged approach will ensure that both individual skills, a classroom culture and personal mindset are all conducive to developing resilience. If this is done, then hopefully our students will develop the key skills and attributes needed to thrive both in and outside of school.

THE ONE ABOUT PHONES AND SLEEP

@inner_drive | www.innerdrive.co.uk

THE STUDY

Many of us use our mobile phones and tablets just before going to and whilst in bed. What impact does this have on our brain? Melatonin, often referred to as "the sleep hormone", is released when it is dark at night and acts as a trigger for us to feel sleepy. But, does the glare from our electronics trick our brain into thinking it is daytime and stop melatonin being fully secreted?

Researchers recently ran a study to find out. Their participants started using their tablets at 11 pm and were told they could engage in whatever task they liked on them, such as reading, gaming or shopping. Then at midnight and at 1 am saliva samples were taken to check their melatonin levels.

THE MAIN FINDINGS

1 **Being on an iPad for one hour at night hardly impacts how much melatonin is released.**

The researchers do note "that usage of self-luminous electronic devices before sleep may disrupt sleep even if melatonin is not supressed. Clearly the tasks themselves may be alerting or stressful *stimuli* that can lead to sleep disruption".

2 **However, being on your iPad for two hours before bed resulted in around 20% less melatonin being released.**

Therefore, they recommend "that these devices be dimmed at night as much as possible in order to minimise melatonin suppression, and that the duration of use be limited prior to bedtime".

Ref: Wood et al, 2013, *Applied Ergonomics*

THE ONE ABOUT PHONES AND SLEEP

 ## RELATED RESEARCH

A recent report found that there are now more mobile phones on the planet than people, with one survey finding that 81% of people report never turning their phone off, even when they are in bed. Another study found that, on average, people check their devices 85 times a day, with many in this study unaware of how often they do so.

More and more research is being done on the link between electronic devices and sleep (#90). One such study found that being on your phone within an hour of bed means that you are almost three times as likely to get less than five hours of sleep. As well as the obvious suggestion to not be on your phone whilst in bed, a different study found another good way to minimise the negative impact was to turn down the backlight and hold your phone more than 12 inches away from your face.

What you do on your phone will also affect the quality and length of sleep. Both social media and constantly replying to messages have been found to increase stress and reduce immunity. If people are going to be on their phone, doing something calming and relaxing on it before bed is certainly advisable.

CLASSROOM IMPLICATIONS

There is obviously only so much that schools and teachers can do about this, as being on electronic devices before bed obviously falls into the category of "out of school hours". However, with lack of sleep and the pressures of social media having such a large impact on how students think, feel and behave at school the next day, it clearly spills into the school arena.

The authors of the study allude to this when they write that their results are "particularly worrisome in populations such as young adults and adolescents, who already tend to be more 'night owls'". Talking to students about the perils of being on their devices too much late at night and the consequences it had on their learning and exam performance makes sense from well-being, pastoral and academic achievement perspectives.

THE ONE ABOUT PICTURES AND WORDS

@inner_drive | www.innerdrive.co.uk

THE STUDY

What do you think would lead to better learning: revising with just words, just pictures, words and then pictures, or words and pictures together? Keen to find out, researchers investigated. Over two experiments, they had students learn about how a bike pump worked using these different techniques. Afterwards, the students took both problem-solving and verbal recall tests.

THE MAIN FINDINGS

Studying with words and pictures together was found to **lead to better learning**. Specifically, on a problem solving test, these students:

✓ Correctly answered over twice as many questions as those who had just revised **with words**.

✓ Correctly answered over **50% more** questions than those who had revised **with just pictures**.

✓ Correctly answered around **50% more** questions than those who had revised by **seeing words followed by pictures**.

Revising with words and pictures together **did not help** when students had to verbally recall what they had studied.

The **difference came when** they had to apply this knowledge to different problems, situations and questions.

Ref: Mayer et al, 1991, *Journal of Educational Psychology*

THE ONE ABOUT PICTURES AND WORDS

RELATED RESEARCH

This research lends support to a memory strategy known as Dual-Coding, which forms a part of Cognitive Load Theory (#89). The authors of the study explain that "this theory predicts that learners will remember and transfer material better if they encode the material both visually and verbally because they have two separate ways of finding the information in their memory".

Therefore, when students study using both words and pictures, this builds both verbal and visual representations of the material, as well as strengthening the connection between the two. This process cements information into long-term memory.

Research into Dual-Coding has found that it enhances memory and learning for primary, secondary and university students. Furthermore, this effect has been found in both laboratory studies and in real-world settings (i.e. in schools) as well as in a range of subjects.

CLASSROOM IMPLICATIONS

Many students use a range of techniques to help them remember large amounts of material. This may include writing out their notes or producing mind-maps. This study, and indeed theory, suggests that this may be an incomplete strategy. As the authors of the study state, "even when instruction involves both words and pictures, our results show that presenting verbal and visual explanations without connecting them is much less helpful than coordinating verbal narration simultaneously with animation". Clearly, doing both simultaneously is far more effective than doing one after the other.

A good way to start using Dual-Coding is to consider what words you could write down to describe the visual graphic or what graphic would capture the core message from the text. Key to this is understanding what type of visuals may go best with the text for each subject or topic. The more congruent the text description and visual graphic are, the more likely it will lead to deeper learning.

THE ONE ABOUT TEACHING OTHERS

@inner_drive | www.innerdrive.co.uk

THE STUDY

What are the best conditions for learning and revision? Does it help motivate people to know that they have an upcoming test? Or is it more beneficial to tell students that they are going to have to teach the material to one of their peers?

These were the questions that researchers sought to answer. Across two experiments, they split 100 students into two groups (teach others vs. prepare for a test). They then measured what they learnt, how much they learnt and how well they did in a test.

THE MAIN FINDINGS

1 Students **who had been expecting to teach** the material to someone else remembered more of the material and **did so in a more efficient way** than those who thought there was going to be a test.

2 In their final exam, those **who had expected to teach someone** performed over **12% better** than those who were working towards the test.

3 As well as remembering more and performing better in tests, **students who thought that they were going to teach someone** were also **more likely to remember** the important information and key topics.

Ref: Nestojko et al, 2014, *Memory and Cognition*

THE ONE ABOUT TEACHING OTHERS

RELATED RESEARCH

Numerous studies have found that when students teach material to other students, they make significant learning gains. In the research, this is known as the Protégé Effect. However, it is worth noting that not all studies have shown this effect. Reasons for these mixed findings may include the increase in anxiety and stress in some students when they must speak in public.

CLASSROOM IMPLICATIONS

What about when students realise they don't have to teach the material? Will this negate the positive impact? The researchers suggest a strategy based on a separate study to help classroom teachers overcome this when they suggest that "perhaps informing the classroom that at least one student among them will be required to teach - but not revealing which student - would prompt all students to prepare as if they will have to teach". This will keep the students "on the hook" and encourage deeper learning.

The researchers note that "instilling an expectation to teach thus seems to be a simple, inexpensive intervention with the potential to increase learning efficiency at home and in the classroom". Why is this effective? They explain:

> Participants expecting to teach put themselves into the mindset of a teacher, leading them to adopt certain effective strategies used by teaching when preparing to teach - such as organizing and weighing the importance of different concepts in the to-be-taught material, focusing on the main points and thinking about how information fits together.

Expecting to teach someone also helps the learner categorise the important information and encourages them to thoroughly go over what they do and don't know in preparation for tough questions. Other reasons why expecting to teach others is so effective are that it encourages self-explanation (prompting detail and depth) and elaborative interrogation (asking yourself "why is this the case?"). Both techniques are regularly associated with higher levels of understanding and memory retention.

THE ONE ABOUT EXPERTS OVERCLAIMING

@inner_drive | www.innerdrive.co.uk

THE STUDY

Many people tend to overestimate their knowledge, skills and abilities. If we believe ourselves to be experts in one area, are we more likely to exaggerate what we actually know? Researchers from Cornell University and Tulane University ran a series of studies to find out.

To give an example of how they tested this, they asked people to rate how familiar they were with a list of key terms. Unbeknownst to those being studied, some of the terms were real and some were fake. For example, in the banking section real terms included "fixed-rate mortgage" and "home equity" and false ones "pre-rated stocks" and "annualized credit".

THE MAIN FINDINGS

1 Over **90% of the participants** claimed to have at least **some knowledge** of some of the made-up phrases.

2 Those **who had done well** in an easy quiz, and thus felt more like an expert about a topic, were subsequently **more likely to overclaim** their knowledge.

3 The more that the participants viewed themselves as an **expert**, the more likely they were to **overclaim their knowledge**.

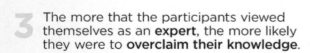

4 This effect of experts overclaiming was found to be **true in a range of studies** and topics, which included science, geography, banking and literature.

5 Even if participants **had been warned** that some of the information they were about to read **was false**, many of them still overclaimed their knowledge about these topics.

Ref: Atir et al, 2015, *Psychological Science*

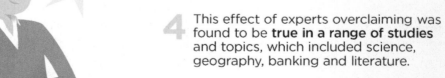

THE ONE ABOUT EXPERTS OVERCLAIMING

RELATED RESEARCH

Other research has shown that people are not very accurate at predicting their own ability levels. To date, this has focused on either novices or people who aren't particularly accomplished at the task at hand overestimating their abilities. This is referred to as the Dunning-Kruger effect (#18).

Further research has also found that the allure of expertise and authority means that people are sometimes seduced by false information. This is one of the reasons why people tend to believe things if it sounds scientific, even if it false (#55).

A different study recently looked at the other costs of being an expert. They found that people who consider themselves to be an expert are also more likely to be closed-minded; refusing to change their original opinion when new and contradictory evidence is presented. This is a form of confirmation bias which occurs because people want to appear to be consistent with their earlier thoughts, beliefs and actions (#45).

CLASSROOM IMPLICATIONS

The authors of this study caution about the pitfalls of experts overclaiming by saying that "a tendency to over claim may discourage individuals from educating themselves in precisely those areas in which they consider themselves knowledgeable and that may be important to them". Steve Jobs, founder of Apple, once alluded to this by advising people to "stay hungry, stay foolish".

If students believe they are already experts, this can lead to them developing a fixed mindset and not seeking out opportunities to develop and improve. Having a fixed mindset has been associated with lower grades, poorer coping skills and reduced mental health (#68). Teachers can help guard against this by consistently setting students challenging work that stretches them and providing feedback that is both regular and focused on concrete steps to get better. This will help protect students against what they say is "the great menace - not ignorance, but the illusion of knowledge".

THE ONE ABOUT THE KÖHLER EFFECT

@inner_drive | www.innerdrive.co.uk

THE STUDY

During the 1920s, German psychologist Otto Köhler found that when two people completed a joint task, the individual performance of the weaker member was better than if they had done it by themselves. This is called the Köhler effect. For example, if mountaineers are tethered together and can only go at the slowest member's pace, this would still be faster than if the slowest person did it by themselves.

Keen to explore in more detail why the Köhler Effect occurs and how to best facilitate it, researchers reviewed all the existing research.

THE MAIN FINDINGS

1 Why the Köhler Effect Works:

Working with someone of higher ability prompts the weaker member to …

- ✔ Try **harder** at the task
- ✔ Set a **higher benchmark** of what is possible
- ✔ Not want to let their team-mate **down**

2 When the Köhler Effect Works Best:

- ✔ When effort levels tangibly and clearly **affect the outcome** of the task
- ✔ When they **feel connected** to the other person
- ✔ When they trust that the other person is **working hard** as well
- ✔ If they get **regular feedback** on individual performance and effort levels
- ✔ If the **ability gap** between pairs is not too big or too small
- ✔ When you **don't always** work with the same person

Ref: Kerr and Hertel, 2011, *Social and Personality Psychology Compass*

THE ONE ABOUT THE KÖHLER EFFECT

RELATED RESEARCH

A recent study found support for the Köhler effect when researchers found that weaker swimmers tended to swim faster when part of a relay team than when they swam by themselves. The stronger members of the team tended to swim at a similar pace to their solo pace. This is a possible reason why mixed-ability classes tend to benefit the weaker students (#36).

The Köhler effect is not to be confused with social loafing, which found that when more group members are added to a task, the individual performance of each member drops. The main difference between the Köhler effect and social loafing is that the former occurs when individual efforts are known, and the weaker member raises their level, whereas if each member's effort level is ambiguous and it is unclear how their effort affects the overall outcome, then social loafing occurs and the performance level of each member drops.

CLASSROOM IMPLICATIONS

A similar sort of effect occurs when teachers place a weaker student next to a stronger one (#20). They hope that it will help raise the effort levels and achievement of the lower-ability child. However, this is slightly different to the Köhler effect, as this effect focuses more on how individuals perform as part of a joint task, not on one by themselves. Still, this theory could potentially be applied to group work and paired presentations.

The researchers do sound a word of warning whilst still conveying a positive tone for the applications of this theory to the classroom, when they conclude by saying:

> Most of the research summarised so far has been conducted under rather artificial conditions in the scientific lab with short-term, ad hoc groups and rather simple tasks . . . nevertheless, there is growing evidence of the Köhler motivation gain effect under more everyday conditions. Thus, although more research is certainly necessary here, we are optimistic that the Köhler motivation gain effect can be found and utilised outside of the scientific lab, contributing broadly to more motivated and successful teamwork.

THE ONE ABOUT THE IKEA EFFECT

@inner_drive | www.innerdrive.co.uk

THE STUDY

The IKEA effect describes how some people overvalue their own ideas, efforts and creations compared to the equivalent done by others. This phenomenon, named after the Swedish furniture store that requires you to assemble your own furniture, partly explains why some people are married to their ideas, over-estimate the quality of their efforts and place more value than others do on the things that they have worked hard on. This may be why some people struggle to, in the words of the animated film *Frozen*, "let it go".

Researchers from Harvard Business School, Tulane University and Duke University ran a series of studies to find out how prevalent the IKEA effect is.

THE MAIN FINDINGS

1 Half the participants built an IKEA piece of furniture, whereas the other half inspected an identical piece once it had already been assembled. They each then estimated the price of it. Those **who had built** the furniture themselves **valued it at 63% more** expensive.

2 People **who had built** their own furniture were also more likely to report **liking their furniture more**.

3 This finding was replicated with participants who **made their own origami**, as they were prepared to pay **nearly five times more** than their counterparts who had not been involved in making it.

4 When comparing **their own piece of work** with that of experts, participants placed a similar value on their work if they had **worked hard** on creating it themselves.

5 Finally, in a separate study, participants were **more likely to place a higher value** on a Lego toy if **a)** it was theirs and **b)** they had built it.

Ref: Norton et al, 2011, *Journal of Consumer Psychology*

THE ONE ABOUT THE IKEA EFFECT

RELATED RESEARCH

There is not a lot of related research on this topic, as it is a relatively new area in psychology. This means that it would be good if these results are tested and replicated again on a different type of sample and in a range of settings.

The nearest related research falls into one of two categories. The first is "effort justification" which found that the worse an initiation into a club, the more members tended to feel that it was worth it. This suggests that they wanted to believe their efforts were justified. This finding, curiously, has been replicated in studies on rats and birds, with both animals preferring food that they had to work hard to get.

The other area in psychology which is similar to the IKEA effect is that of confirmation bias. This states that people tend to prefer people and ideas that they have previously agreed with. The need to feel consistent with our prior activities drives how we then feel about a new situation.

CLASSROOM IMPLICATIONS

There obviously is nothing wrong with valuing your own efforts and hard work. The problem comes with the disconnect between what we see and what others see. The researchers summed this up well by using the metaphor of selling your house: "for instance, people may see the improvements they have made to their homes - such as the brick walkway they laid by hand - as increasing the value of the house far more than buyers, who only see a shoddily built walkway".

This helps explain why some people have a hard time letting go of their "brilliant idea". This leads to them persisting long after they should quit and come up with a better one. It is the gambler's equivalent of throwing good money after bad. This can be compounded by the frustration when others do not see the value of your suggestions. Although resilience and persistence are clearly admirable traits, knowing that we have a bias to our own work, ideas and effort can help save everyone time and money if we are able to accurately assess the value of the "brilliant idea".

THE ONE ABOUT PARENTAL BELIEFS

@inner_drive | www.innerdrive.co.uk

THE STUDY

Maths is a subject that students tend to have very strong opinions about one way or another. One of the most important and interesting studies on parental beliefs and their impact on how students view their maths ability was conducted over 30 years ago.

In this study, researchers from The University of Michigan administered a series of questionnaires to children aged 10–15 years old and their parents. They wanted to see how powerful parental attitudes and expectations were and if these varied between parents of sons and parents of daughters.

THE MAIN FINDINGS

1 A child's opinion of their own ability and expectation of future success was **heavily shaped** by what their parents thought about them.

This actually had more impact than the child's previous grades in that subject. Essentially, they **believe their parents more** than their grades.

2 Out of the two, the **attitudes and beliefs of mothers** towards their child's educational abilities had **more impact** than the father's.

3 Parents of daughters thought that **maths was harder** for their child and that they would have to **work harder to do well** in it compared to parents of sons. This belief was held by both mothers and fathers.

4 Parents of sons thought **advanced maths** was more important for their child than parents of daughters.

Ref: Parson et al, 1982, *Child Development*

THE ONE ABOUT PARENTAL BELIEFS

 RELATED RESEARCH

Recent research has focused on which parental attitudes and behaviours are most likely to help students get better grades. The most significant by far were having high academic expectations (#11). This included how important parents saw school, their attitude towards teachers and the overall value of education. Other strategies included regular communication, encouraging good reading habits (#54) and setting clear boundaries and structure for managing homework and social leisure time.

Previous evidence suggests that parents (and teachers) tend to have subconscious bias towards their beliefs about what different genders can achieve in school, with several studies finding higher expectations for boys once they are in the latter stages of their education. Indeed, it is interesting to note how one study (#19) found that parents were more than twice as likely to praise their sons for their effort compared with their daughters. Perhaps this explains why other studies have found that girls think they have to work harder at maths than boys do, even though both girls and boys report spending similar amounts of time doing their homework.

CLASSROOM IMPLICATIONS

The authors of the study point out that the main finding of their study is that "parental beliefs are even more critical mediators than the child's own maths performance" and that "by attributing their daughter's achievements to hard work and their son's to high ability, parents may be teaching their sons and daughters to draw different inferences regarding their achievement abilities".

This means that, each time a parent says that their child "isn't a maths person", it can have a very serious and negative impact on the child's beliefs about their maths potential. This suggests that working closely with parents to help raise student aspirations, expectations and performances would be a productive strategy. Parents evenings are a prime opportunity for parents not only to discuss how their children are getting on, but also for teachers to inform parents of this sort of research and the extent that their words affect their children's academic performance.

THE ONE ABOUT MOTIVATION

@inner_drive | www.innerdrive.co.uk

THE STUDY

If you had to learn a new topic that was taught in the most boring of ways, what do you think would be the best way to motivate yourself? Researchers from the University of Iowa and the University of Oklahoma divided students into four groups to find out. The first was not given a reason to try hard. The second was told about an important test on the topic. The third group was told that trying hard was what they "should" do as it was expected of them, and finally the fourth group was told that they would be learning a new skill that would help them in the future.

THE MAIN FINDINGS

The fourth group, with an emphasis on developing skills for their future, performed better on a range of measures. Specifically:

✓ They **rated the lesson as more important.** In some cases, this difference was **up to 25% more** than in the other three groups.

✓ They had **higher levels of self-determination,** that is, **an increase** in more internal motivation.

✓ They were **far more likely** to put in more effort in the lesson. Knowing that there **would be a test,** that it was expected of them or no reason resulted in a lot less effort.

Effort vs Why

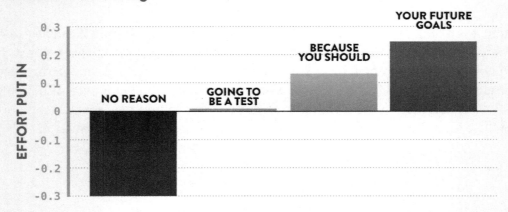

Ref: Reeve et al, 2004, *Motivation and Emotion*

THE ONE ABOUT MOTIVATION

RELATED RESEARCH

There has been a plethora of research on how best to enhance motivation (#26, #44). One fascinating paper found that individual motivation can be improved if the person felt that they had a reasonable amount of choice over what they did or how they did it, if they knew why they were doing it, and if quality feedback was offered. Other research has shown that, if people feel that they are getting better or learning new things, then their motivation levels will remain constant and high.

Other ways to boost motivation levels can be found in research around goal-setting. If done correctly, in a way that is both challenging and realistic as well as process-focused, it can increase concentration, class participation and the likelihood of students choosing challenging tasks. As a result, initial performance improves, which creates a positive cycle of even higher motivation levels and better subsequent performances.

CLASSROOM IMPLICATIONS

Helping some students maintain their motivation levels is a problem that every teacher encounters. Instead of seeing motivation as something you give someone, it is better to see motivation as something that you can help develop. This research gives an indication of how this can be done. Clearly, emphasising the importance of an upcoming test can help provide a short-term boost before an event, but doing so is unlikely to help foster the intrinsic motivation needed for students to learn a large amount of material over a sustained period of time.

The authors of this study do note that "it would be a misrepresentation of our findings to conclude that simply telling another person that an activity is useful will lead them to identify with its personal value". Understanding why an activity is important and helping students identify how it will be of direct help to them, as well as how it will help them achieve their goals, is a much more effective approach to facilitating meaningful motivation.

THE ONE ABOUT STUDENT DAYDREAMING

@inner_drive | www.innerdrive.co.uk

THE STUDY

You feel that you are delivering a great lesson, but are your students really paying attention? Sometimes it is obvious, but sometimes it is hard to spot when students are daydreaming. So, how prevalent is mind wandering in class, when is it most likely to occur and what are the costs of daydreaming?

Researchers from the University of Waterloo in Canada tracked 154 students over the course of a 12-week term. At various random stages in their lectures, they were asked to rate their levels of concentration and report on what they had just been focusing on. Their results allow us to know more than ever before how much attention students really pay in class.

THE MAIN FINDINGS

1 Students' minds **wandered for a third** of their lectures. **14%** of the time was spent unintentionally daydreaming and **20%** of the time students actively chose to think about things other than the lecture.

2 Attention levels **don't linearly decrease** during a 50-minute lecture. Interestingly, attention levels were actually **lower in the third quarter** than they were in the fourth quarter.

3 Students' minds were most likely to wander on **a Monday** and **a Friday**. They were at their **most focused** on **Wednesdays**.

The researchers speculated that this was due to students either worrying about the upcoming week or being distracted by thoughts about the weekend.

4 During lessons towards the end of term, students were far **more likely** to report being distracted in their lessons. One possible reason for this could be that **their minds were on upcoming exams** and the potential consequences of not doing well in the exam.

5 Unsurprisingly, the more students reported daydreaming, the worse they did in their exams. This was **true for all students** regardless of their previous academic performance.

Ref: Wammes et al, 2016, *Scholarship of Teaching and Learning in Psychology*

THE ONE ABOUT STUDENT DAYDREAMING

RELATED RESEARCH

One of the first reported studies in this area, in the 1970s, had students report on what they were focusing on every time their teacher rang a bell. Amazingly, students reported not focusing on the task at hand in lessons for the same amount of time as the students in this study over 40 years later. Both sets of students reported focusing on something that wasn't to do with the lesson 33% of the time.

Other research has found similar levels of student inattention. Evidence from other studies also highlights how concentration levels tend to dip after thirty minutes, and that excessive classroom decorations can be distracting for younger students, which reduces their rate of learning (#93).

What can be done to reduce the time spent not focusing on the task at hand? Some researchers have hypothesised a link between motivation and daydreaming in which increasing the former reduces the latter. Indeed, the authors of the study note that:

> Mind wandering of the intentional sort might be curtailed through interventions that increase students' motivation to perform, or their perceived value of attending to the lecture material. One way to increase students' motivation to attend might be to include quiz questions in the lecture, with the accuracy of the students' responses counting toward their final grade.

CLASSROOM IMPLICATIONS

What can a teacher do differently given the results of this study? Given that students are more likely to be distracted on Mondays and Fridays, the authors of the study suggest that "instructors might consider presenting a greater volume of material, or presenting the most important material midweek".

Beyond shifting around when you teach certain topics, there are many proven factors and behaviours associated with better concentration. These include getting a good night's sleep regularly, eating breakfast every morning, drinking plenty of water, regular exercise, taking notes in class (#32) and turning mobile phones off. If we can explicitly teach these to students, we can arm them with a wider range of strategies that they can employ to increase their focus during lessons.

THE ONE ABOUT BANNING MOBILE PHONES

@inner_drive | www.innerdrive.co.uk

THE STUDY

Should schools ban mobile phones? As with all technology, there are pros and cons. Mobile phones offer the opportunity to connect people and ideas as well as offering a range of revision apps. However, social media and games may distract focus away from learning.

Taking a long-term and evidence-based approach, researchers measured the impact that banning mobile phones had over a number of years. They tracked schools that enforced a ban, those that weakly enforced a ban and those that had no ban. They tracked what effect it had on student performance in their GCSEs.

THE MAIN FINDINGS

1 Students who attended a **school that banned mobile phones** received, on average, a **6.4%** **increase** in their exam results.

2 This effect was **most pronounced** for struggling students, with those who had previously been low-achieving receiving a **boost of 14%** on average.

3 The most able students **did not gain any increase** from the mobile phone banning policy, but they also did not suffer any negative ones.

4 Students who attended a school that banned mobile phones were **more likely** to go on to achieve **at least five GCSEs** of grades A*–C.

5 Schools that reported **only weakly enforcing the ban** did not receive as much of a boost to their exam results as those schools which enforced it thoroughly.

6 The **longer a school had banned mobile phones**, the larger the boost students got in their exam results.

Ref: Beland and Murphy, 2015, *CEP Discussion Paper No 1350*

THE ONE ABOUT BANNING MOBILE PHONES

RELATED RESEARCH

Excessive mobile phone use has been associated with a reduction in concentration (#30), an increase in the fear of missing out, heightened anxiety and stress, as well as hindering both memory and sleep (#40). Within classrooms, there is evidence to suggest that technology may not be the powerful answer that many were hoping for. For example, students who take notes on electronic devices remember less about their lesson and perform worse in exams (#72).

Likewise, even when given explicit instructions on how to use technology, many report reverting to playing games and browsing online. Finally, a separate study found that students who report being on their phones a lot go on to get worse grades. This finding was found to be true for all students, regardless of gender or previous grade average.

CLASSROOM IMPLICATIONS

Schools from around the world have started banning mobile phones. These include many in France, America and England. This study suggests that they have been right to do so. As the authors of this study note, "highly multipurpose technology, such as mobile phones, can have a negative impact on productivity through distraction. Schools that restrict access to mobile phones subsequently experience an improvement in test scores".

They do conclude their study with a slight caveat, which is that they "do not discount the possibility that mobile phones could be a useful learning tool if their use is structured properly". However, given that at this stage it is not clear what this proper structure looks like, it seems prudent to advise that when it comes to the banning of mobile phones, the positives of doing so outweigh the negatives.

This strategy may well be met with objections by both students and parents. Common arguments against doing so are that a) they are used as a safety device that allows students to get in touch with parents after school or b) that as this technology is part of the 21st century, schools should embrace it. The former argument can be countered as mobile phones can be turned on at the end of the school day, whereas the latter argument falls short given that, overall, mobile phones don't lead to better learning.

THE ONE ABOUT GOING FOR A WALK

@inner_drive | www.innerdrive.co.uk

THE STUDY

The classical Greek physician Hippocrates once stated that "if you are in a bad mood, go for a walk. If you are still in a bad mood, go for another walk". So, does going for a walk actually help improve mood? What if you know you have to do a really hard and boring task afterwards? And how short does a "short walk" have to be for people to get any psychological benefit from it?

Across three experiments, researchers Jeffrey Miller and Zlatan Krizan of Iowa State University sought to find out.

THE MAIN FINDINGS

1 Students who went for **a 12-minute walk** reported **feeling much better** (i.e. around 20% increase) than those who had spent **the same amount of time sitting down** looking at photos. This included feelings of happiness, attentiveness and confidence.

2 Students who knew they had to do a **hard and boring task afterwards**, still **had a positive mood boost** as a result of their walk. Those who had been sitting down instead **did not**.

3 Participants who took part in a really short walk, **lasting only 5 minutes**, still got the benefits and reported **feeling better** afterwards.

4 Having a walking break **doesn't even need to involve going outside** to feel the benefits. Students who went for a short walk inside felt **better afterwards**. Students who stood still or sat down reported **feeling worse**.

Ref: Miller and Krizan, 2016, *Emotion*

THE ONE ABOUT GOING FOR A WALK

 ## RELATED RESEARCH

There is a lot of emerging research that highlights the many and varied benefits of physical activity. For example, researchers have found that those who regularly exercise cope better with stressful situations and report feeling more focused and alert on days that they have exercised. Likewise, a recent study found that students who exercised up to four hours after a lesson were later able to recall and retain more information compared with those who did not.

The long-term effects of exercise now are also well-known. These include, but are not limited to, enhanced cognitive functions, physical health benefits and feeling more refreshed. Where you go for a walk may also matter, with recent evidence suggesting that those who do so in natural environments get an extra boost compared with those who do so in urban environments (#59). This is because urban environments require individuals to stay alert and, because of that, some of the positive psychological impact of going for a walk may be negated.

CLASSROOM IMPLICATIONS

This study could prove useful in helping students enhance their mood. This may be why going for "learning walks" or breaking up study sessions with a quick stroll may help. So, why don't students do this more? The researchers note that "people may underestimate the extent to which just getting off their couch and going for a walk will benefit their mood as they focus on momentarily perceived barriers rather than eventual mood benefits".

The results from this study could not be clearer, in that "walking has powerful and ongoing consequences on our mental states, and these should be harnessed to improve wellbeing and performance". What is good to know is that this evidence shows that it does not have to be a long walk. Even 5-10 minutes could provide just the pick-me-up that students need for the rest of the day.

THE ONE ABOUT STRESS MINDSETS

@inner_drive | www.innerdrive.co.uk

THE STUDY

It is a myth that stress is always bad. It is probably more accurate to portray it in terms of the "Goldilocks effect" – too much or too little is not helpful. If there is enough to motivate a person and yet not so much that it hinders useful behaviours, then clear thinking and performance can improve.

Central to this may be how individuals interpret stress. Some view stress as always being a bad thing, whereas others view it as having some potential benefit. This is known as your "stress mindset". Researchers from Yale University ran a study to test if a "stress mindset" was actually a real thing and if so, what impact it had.

THE MAIN FINDINGS

1 Stress can be viewed in **one of two ways**: either with the potential to **enhance or debilitate** performance.

2 Our **stress mindset** can be developed. Learning how it can help us is key.

3 Those who view stress as being helpful reported:
- ✔ **Feeling better**
- ✔ **Better work performance**
- ✔ **Being more likely to seek out feedback**

4 If participants had **high levels of cortisol**, the stress hormone, then a belief that stress can be good for you **helped lower it**.

If participants **had low levels of cortisol**, then believing stress can be good for you **helped raise it**. Essentially, it helped participants find their **sweet spot**.

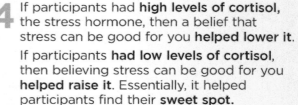

Ref: Crum et al, 2013, *Journal of Personality and Social Psychology*

THE ONE ABOUT STRESS MINDSETS

RELATED RESEARCH

Research has identified that stress plays a role in the six main causes of death (heart disease, accidents, cancer, liver disease, lung ailments and suicide). It is also associated with sick days and a reduction in productivity, depression and general reduction in performance. However, it is worth noting that, in evolutionary terms, stress played a key role in our survival, as it helped our ancestors run faster and think quicker under pressure. A little bit of stress can also help people learn and perform more effectively (#60).

The benefits of stress have been studied from two different viewpoints, physiologically and psychologically. From a physiological perspective, there is evidence that shows that an appropriate amount of stress elicits the release of certain hormones that can help repair cells which can make the body stronger and healthier. Likewise, several researchers have found that individuals report having more meaning to their lives, develop resilience, a new sense of perspective and better relationships because they experienced stressful situations. This has been dubbed "stress related growth".

CLASSROOM IMPLICATIONS

This study does not suggest that more stress is better or that there are no downsides to experiencing stress. Instead, what the authors of the study point out is that "the findings of these studies indicate that people can be primed to adopt a stress-is-enhancing mindset, which can have positive consequences relating to improved health and work performance".

This suggests that, during times of heightened stress – for example, exam time or during public speaking – teachers need to help students develop three things. Firstly, a larger skill and knowledge base from which to draw. The more competent someone is at something, the less likely they are to become stressed whilst doing it. Secondly, self-regulation and metacognitive skills can help them deliver their best under pressure. Third and finally, that one's stress mindset is not set in stone. Focusing on how to interpret both the event itself and one's attitude to stress can significantly reduce one's negative feelings whilst concurrently boosting performance.

THE ONE ABOUT HOW TO GIVE BETTER FEEDBACK

@inner_drive | www.innerdrive.co.uk

THE STUDY

Given the amount of time, energy and effort that is invested into giving feedback, it would be handy to know what good feedback actually looks like. Researchers John Hattie and Helen Timperley from the University of Auckland conducted a thorough review of the existing research. Their findings offer simple tips, strategies and guidelines on what may work best.

THE MAIN FINDINGS

1 In order to be most effective, feedback must answer three questions:

Where am I going?
This makes your goal crystal clear.

How am I going?
This gives an indication of progress.

Where to next?
Perhaps the most important question, as it focuses on strategies needed in order to improve.

2 Researchers also identified four types of feedback and commented on their effectiveness:

Feedback about the person
This is **the least effective** as it leads to labelling, such as "you are smart" or "you are not a maths person", neither of which is particularly helpful.

Feedback about the task
This is the most common and provides information on whether the work was correct. **This is often effective** if students had a faulty interpretation of what was needed.

Feedback about the process
Provides information on how the students did the task. It prompts them to search out more information and **often leads to deeper learning** than just feedback on the task.

Feedback about self-regulation
This covers how well students monitored their performance, regulated their actions and tweaked their strategies. This is more **effective for novice learners**.

Ref: Hattie and Timperley, 2007, *Review of Educational Research*

THE ONE ABOUT HOW TO GIVE BETTER FEEDBACK

RELATED RESEARCH

One famous review on feedback studies found that 38% of feedback interventions actually do more harm than good (#25). As a result, this topic has been studied extensively (#97). It is just too important to get wrong or to not know the potential implications.

One study found that a quarter of teenager students prefer to be praised loudly and publicly, whereas two-thirds of students preferred it if the teacher did it quietly and discreetly. Interestingly, 10% of students preferred it if a teacher said nothing at all. Several other researchers have found that, if feedback is merged with praise, it can have a detrimental effect if delivered in the presence of one's friends who do not value hard work and doing well at school.

A different study confirmed these findings and found that students preferred praise for their efforts over praise for their natural abilities. This sort of feedback is associated with students enjoying a task more, enhancing their resilience and choosing more challenging tasks in the future (#5).

CLASSROOM IMPLICATIONS

For better tips on giving good feedback, the authors of the study recommend two separate but inter-related strategies. The first is that "feedback is more effective when it provides information on correct rather than incorrect responses and when it builds on changes from previous trials". The second is that feedback is "more effective when there are perceived low rather than high levels of threat to self-esteem, presumably because low-threat conditions allow attention to be paid to the feedback".

This research paper is gold dust for teachers, given how much time is spent in the classroom giving students feedback. These strategies suggest that it is about quality rather than quantity. Or, as the researchers state, "simply providing more feedback is not the answer, because it is necessary to consider the nature of the feedback, the timing, and how a student receives this feedback".

THE ONE ABOUT ABOUT SELF-TALK

@inner_drive | www.innerdrive.co.uk

THE STUDY

What do Donald Trump, Zlatan Ibrahimovic, Julius Caesar and Elmo from *Sesame Street* all have in common? They are all known to talk about themselves in the third person. One famous example of this was when Zlatan Ibrahimovic was invited to a trial at Arsenal. He replied, "Zlatan doesn't do auditions".

But what impact does how you talk to yourself have on how you think, feel and behave? Does talking in the first person (i.e. "I thought that ...") differ when compared to non-first person (i.e. "You thought that ..." or using your own name in the third person)? Researchers had students talk to themselves in one of these two ways and then put them in a range of situations that included recalling bad events, meeting someone for the first time and giving a presentation in front of their peers.

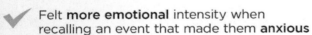

THE MAIN FINDINGS

People who talked to themselves in the first person compared to non-first person

✔ Felt **more emotional** intensity when recalling an event that made them **anxious**

✔ Felt **more emotional** intensity when recalling an event that made them **angry**

✔ Were rated as **appearing more nervous** and **performed worse** in social interactions

✔ Were **less likely** to make a good **first impression**

✔ Experienced more **shame, embarrassment** and **negative moods** during a public speaking task

✔ **Performed worse** at the public speaking task

✔ Were **more likely** to see upcoming stressful events as a **threat**

✔ Were **more likely** to **worry** about upcoming stressful events

Ref: Kross et al, 2014, Journal of Personality and Social Psychology

THE ONE ABOUT SELF-TALK

 ## RELATED RESEARCH

The area of self-talk is one of the most well-researched and robust areas in cognitive psychology (#24, #64). How one talks to oneself has been found to affect one's mindset, motivation, resilience, creativity, concentration, emotional control and metacognitive abilities (#84). For example, one study found that participants who asked themselves questions (i.e. "Will I do well?") solved far more anagrams than those who had declared they would succeed (i.e. "I will do well"). One possible reason for this is asking yourself questions prompts the brain to answer questions, acting as a call to action (#28).

Other studies have found that telling yourself what to do in a helpful and constructive manner improves attention and performance under pressure. This technique has also been found to help students improve self-control as well as to boost their planning and preparation before an important task. Finally, talking to oneself in an upbeat and energised way has been found to help people block out potentially distracting thoughts. This helps improve performance in which a large amount of effort and resilience is required.

CLASSROOM IMPLICATIONS

This research shows the numerous benefits of developing how students talk to themselves. The authors conclude their findings by stating that

> We are not accustomed to people referring to themselves using their own name - the current findings suggest that doing so promotes self-distancing; enhances people's ability to regulate their thoughts, feelings and behaviours under social stress; and leads them to appraise social-anxiety-provoking events in more challenging and less threatening terms.

Given the advantages associated with this type of self-talk, it is interesting to consider how little time is actually spent on helping students develop a healthy and helpful self-narrative. A few simple tweaks can really have a big impact on how students think, feel and behave. Given that self-regulation and emotional management are key day-to-day skills (#37), helping students develop their self-talk skills promises to be a simple, cheap and effective strategy to boost their well-being and achievement.

#54

THE ONE ABOUT PARENTS AND READING

@inner_drive | www.innerdrive.co.uk

THE STUDY

Parents are often advised to read to their children as part of a night-time routine. But is there a way that they can do this to best develop the reading skills of their children?

Researchers tracked children ages 4 to 6 years old for several years and measured how much parents reported reading to them, what type of reading activities they participated in and then measured key literacy skills. The researchers defined two distinct reading practices that parents participate in. These were informal interactions (i.e. reading storybooks) and formal interactions (i.e. teaching different letter names and sounds). They tested to see if these two different strategies played an important and distinct role in developing literacy skills.

THE MAIN FINDINGS

1 **"Informal interactions"**, such as reading storybooks, had a **positive impact** a year later on their child's ability to:

✔ **Understand words and sentences**

✔ **Use a wider range of vocabulary**

✔ **Develop listening comprehension skills**

2 **Teaching children** about letters, words and sentences during reading (i.e. formal interactions) was also found to play a role in **developing early literacy skills**.

3 The **amount of books** that children were exposed to by age 6 was a **positive predictor** of their reading ability two years later.

Ref: Senechal and LeFevre, 2002, *Child Development*

THE ONE ABOUT PARENTS AND READING

 ## RELATED RESEARCH

The positive effects of reading storybooks to children have long been established. It is interesting to note that research indicates that many children enjoy this time with their parents, with many children often initiating joint reading time together. Children's interest in reading books has been linked to their reading abilities at a younger age. This suggests that if we want to develop a love of reading in our children, it is important that we help them develop their competence and confidence levels early.

One related study found that it is not just the quantity of reading that parents do with their child that matters but, rather, the quality of the interactions during this activity. This includes both describing what is happening and putting on a little performance whilst doing so.

CLASSROOM IMPLICATIONS

A recent study found that students who are behind on their reading age at 9 years old are four times less likely to graduate high school. This emphasises the importance of helping students develop these key skills early. Essentially, if children come to school without the tools needed to learn, although it is possible for them to catch up, it makes their educational experience far more challenging.

Educating parents that a combination of both formal and informal interactions during reading activities can help play a big role in their child's eventual reading ability. This emphasis on both quality and quantity, as well as varying the types of activities, can offer parents a good starting point. Pointing parents in the right direction in terms of types of books and equipping them with good questions and prompts during reading time with their children should help.

THE ONE ABOUT THE SEDUCTION OF NEUROSCIENCE

@inner_drive | www.innerdrive.co.uk

THE STUDY

There is a growing trend in society to want to explain human behaviour and experiences through the lens of neuroscience. This is evident with neuroscientific sounding explanations. But how seductive and powerful are they?

To test this, researchers from Yale University ran a series of cunning experiments. They explained several psychological topics to participants. Some of these explanations were accurate and some were false. Within the explanations, some had supplementary neuroscientific sounding information whilst others did not. The participants then had to rate how satisfying they found the explanations.

THE MAIN FINDINGS

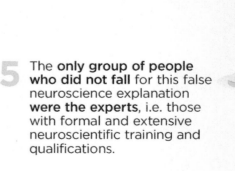

1 People are more likely to rate explanations about psychology and learning as **more satisfying** if they are accompanied by **neuroscientific jargon.**

2 Even if the neuroscientific information **was false or made up**, most people still thought this information **was good.**

3 This effect, which could be termed **"the seduction of neuroscience"**, is most pronounced when the original explanation is considered **weak** and **of a low standard.**

4 It turns out that **novices** and those with **some neuroscientific knowledge** are **both likely to fall** for the erroneous brain images and false explanations.

5 The **only group of people who did not fall** for this false neuroscience explanation **were the experts**, i.e. those with formal and extensive neuroscientific training and qualifications.

Ref: Weisberg et al, 2008, *Journal of Cognitive Neuroscience*

THE ONE ABOUT THE SEDUCTION OF NEUROSCIENCE

 ## RELATED RESEARCH

There are many techniques that can be used to sway how accurate people think an explanation is for something. For example, one study found that people were more likely to believe explanations that were longer. Another study found that people preferred reasoning that they found to be satisfying, over reasoning that was accurate.

Other evidence suggests that images of the brain carry weight and help sway people's reasoning. This may be because they have an air of authority about them or because the striking visual images capture attention. This has been termed "seductive details", which occurs when interesting and stand-out information is included in an argument even if it is not relevant to the topic at hand. This has been found to divert people's focus away from the important parts of an explanation and distract them with interesting but irrelevant information.

CLASSROOM IMPLICATIONS

The authors of this study note that "the presence of neuroscience information may be seen as a strong marker of a good explanation, regardless of the actual status of that information within the explanation . . . people may therefore uncritically accept any explanation containing neuroscience information". They warn that "irrelevant neuroscience information can be seductive - it can have much more of an impact on participants' judgement than it ought to" and cite another research paper which best sums up this area when stating that "pictures of blobs on brains seduce one into thinking that we can now directly observe psychological processes".

They conclude their study by warning that "because it is unlikely that the popularity of neuroscience findings in the public sphere will wane any time soon, we see in the current results more reasons for caution when applying neuroscientific findings to social issues". With a growing interest in schools on how the brain works, teachers and policy makers are advised to take headline findings with a pinch of salt, to not be seduced by brain scan images and to really dig deep into the nuances of potential research findings.

THE ONE ABOUT DEADLINES, CHOICE AND PROCRASTINATION

@inner_drive | www.innerdrive.co.uk

THE STUDY

Are students prepared to set self-imposed deadlines to help themselves overcome their procrastination? Do they set effective deadlines for themselves? And do these self-imposed deadlines actually help improve their performance?

To investigate these questions, researchers divided students into two groups. In the first group, students got to set their own deadlines for three pieces of work. In the other, the teacher set the deadlines and did so evenly over the course of the term. They then tracked how the students got on.

In a follow-up study, they replicated these conditions with students who had to proofread someone else's work. Again, some of these students chose their own deadlines whereas others had deadlines imposed upon them.

THE MAIN FINDINGS

1 Perhaps unsurprisingly, a lot of students decided to submit all three assignments in the **last week of term**, with **27%** of students deciding to submit all three assignment on the **very last day** of term.

2 Students who chose their own deadlines got lower marks than those who had been set the deadlines by their teacher.

3 The biggest difference between the **student-set deadline** and **teacher-set deadline** was for the third and final piece of work, with almost **10%** difference between the two groups.

This was because if students handed in all three pieces of work at the end of the term, **they were often left with too little time** to do the final assignment.

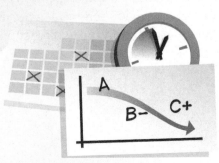

4 Students **preferred to choose their own deadlines**, even though this ended up leading to worse overall grades.

5 Students who were set deadlines reported **spending more time on the tasks** compared to students who got to choose their own deadlines.

Ref: Ariely and Weternbroch, 2002, *Psychological Science*

THE ONE ABOUT DEADLINES, CHOICE AND PROCRASTINATION

 ## RELATED RESEARCH

Procrastination is a big problem for many students. Previous research has found that 75% of students consider themselves procrastinators, with 50% doing so regularly and to a level that is considered problematic. One reason why students may procrastinate is because people are often poor at predicting how long a task will take and will often underestimate the time needed to complete it. This is known as the "planning fallacy" (#3).

Other research has focused on not just the cost of procrastination but on the behaviours and thought processes associated with it. This includes low self-esteem, irrational beliefs, a high fear of failure, depression, poor study habits and too much time spent daydreaming about being successful (#63). Furthermore, those who procrastinate have been found to be more stressed and likely to be ill nearer a deadline, often culminating in lower results.

The results of this study support the findings of one of the largest-ever reviews on procrastination. In that review, the researcher noted that short, regular deadlines would help, as "it has long been observed that the further away an event is, the less impact it has on peoples' decisions".

CLASSROOM IMPLICATIONS

The researchers of the study succinctly summed up their findings when they concluded that "self-imposed deadlines did not enhance performance as much as externally imposed, evenly spaced deadlines". Why might this be the case? One reason they suggest is that "it is possible that students in the free-choice section, compared with those in the no-choice section, treated these deadlines as less binding because they were self-imposed".

Teachers can use this research to help ensure their students stay focused and on track, especially as they get older and need to do more independent study and research. Even if students have to take more responsibility for when, where and how they do their homework, they can still be aided by teachers breaking down large tasks into small chunks with regular deadlines for submitting draft pieces of work.

THE ONE ABOUT SMART REPUTATIONS

@inner_drive | www.innerdrive.co.uk

THE STUDY

When students do something well or are successful, it is almost second nature to say something like "well done, you are such a smart boy" or "you're such a clever girl". But is there a cost of praising someone for their intelligence? What implications does this have for future tasks?

Researchers from universities in China, America and Canada recently collaborated on a study to find out. Working with 243 young children, they told half of them that they had a reputation for being smart. All the students played a guessing game where there was an opportunity to cheat, by peeking at the answer when the experimenter stepped outside the room. They wanted to see if having a smart reputation influenced the students' decision to cheat or not.

THE MAIN FINDINGS

1 **61%** of the students **with a smart reputation cheated** in the game, whereas **only** **41%** of the other students did.

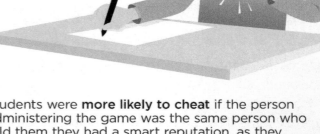

2 Even students as young as three years old were **more likely to cheat** if they believed others thought that they were smart.

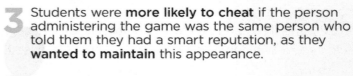

3 Students were **more likely to cheat** if the person administering the game was the same person who told them they had a smart reputation, as they **wanted to maintain** this appearance.

4 **Boys were more likely to cheat** than girls, regardless of whether they had a smart reputation or not.

Ref: Zhao et al, 2017, *Developmental Science*

THE ONE ABOUT SMART REPUTATIONS

RELATED RESEARCH

Previous research found that students understand their reputations by the age of 5. This study suggests that it may be even earlier. It is interesting to consider that other research has found that children under the age of 7 worry less about how smart they are compared with older children. This would suggest that adults are more fascinated by how intelligent a young child is than the actual child is themselves.

Other evidence suggests that students who are praised for their natural ability or intelligence were more likely to give up on difficult tasks, enjoy the tasks less, perform worse and lie about how well they had done (#5). This has also been associated with lower self-esteem and higher levels of stress (#68).

The finding in this study that boys cheated more than girls is consistent with research in economics and psychology that found that adult males are more likely to cheat and act dishonestly than females. However, the reason for this is currently unclear and is still being investigated.

CLASSROOM IMPLICATIONS

The authors state that "providing positive information to children about their intellectual ability can have unintended negative consequences". This is because telling them that they are smart may "motivate them to cheat in pursuit of personal gain". What starts with the good intention of boosting a child's morale can quickly become a weight on their shoulders.

It is important that we keep students focused on improving themselves, rather than worrying about proving themselves. If their perception of winning or being smart is more important to them than getting better, then they are likely to take short-cuts and cheat to maintain that reputation. This can be the difference between students not wanting to make mistakes and them wanting to improve, between not wanting to lose rather than wanting to learn and between self-protecting behaviours versus self-enhancing ones. By praising their processes and not their innate ability, we can help students navigate through challenging times.

THE ONE ABOUT EMOTIONS AND ACHIEVEMENT

@inner_drive | www.innerdrive.co.uk

THE STUDY

Does how well students do at school affect how they feel? Or does how they feel affect how well they do? Or is it both? Eager to answer these questions, researchers from Germany, England, Australia and Japan tracked over 2,000 teenage students from 42 schools for five years to find out.

THE MAIN FINDINGS

1 The relationship between positive emotions and grades work both ways. The more students **enjoyed maths and took pride** in their work, the **higher** their grades were. Likewise, the **more success** that students had, the more **pride and enjoyment** they felt.

2 The **more negative** emotions that students experienced, the **worse their grades** were. These included:

- ✔ **Anger**
- ✔ **Anxiety**
- ✔ **Shame**
- ✔ **Boredom**
- ✔ **Hopelessness**

3 The most powerful **predictor of negative grades** was the amount of anxiety and hopelessness that students felt. Again, this **worked both ways**, with consistent failure increasing the intensity of these negative emotions.

4 The researchers also found that **girls reported lower** enjoyment, lower pride, more boredom, higher anxiety, more shame and more hopelessness in maths classes than boys.

Ref: Pekrun et al, 2017, *Child Development*

THE ONE ABOUT EMOTIONS AND ACHIEVEMENT

 ## RELATED RESEARCH

The finding from this study that emotions and achievement have a reciprocal relationship (i.e. that it works both ways) supports previous research in this area. For example, several studies have found that students who experience test anxiety are more likely to perform worse which, in turn, makes them more likely to experience more test anxiety – in other words, a negative feedback loop.

It is interesting that this study focused on emotional reactions towards maths, as this is consistently one of the subjects that students report having very strong feelings about. Female students regularly report less enjoyment and more anxiety in maths than boys do, even when they achieve similar results. This difference is not down to biological variation, but a combination of the different type of praise boys and girls receive and their attributions for the causes of their failures (#19, #46).

CLASSROOM IMPLICATIONS

The findings from this study suggest that a two-pronged approach should be taken when working with students. The first is to help them manage and nurture their emotions so that they can get better grades. The second is to develop the abilities and knowledge of students so that they will experience better emotions. By only focusing on one aspect, such as improving their well-being or just improving their maths expertise, we miss an opportunity to help them develop. A combination of the two is required.

The authors of this study state that their findings "suggest that educators, administrators and parents alike should consider intensifying efforts that strengthen adolescents' positive emotions and minimize their negative emotions". They suggest that this can be done by "providing students with opportunities to experience success (e.g. using intrapersonal standards to evaluate achievement; emphasising mastery over competition goals) may help to promote positive emotions and prevent negative emotions".

THE ONE ABOUT INTERACTING WITH NATURE

@inner_drive | www.innerdrive.co.uk

THE STUDY

Researchers from the University of Michigan ran two experiments to find out if interacting with nature during a study break improved students' feelings, concentration and memory.

To test this, they first looked at whether where you go for a walk has an effect. In a second study, students spent their study break either looking at photos of nature or of busy city centres. The researchers then compared the two groups.

THE MAIN FINDINGS

In the first study, students took their study break by either going for a 50-minute walk in a park or in a busy urban area. The researchers found that:

1 Students who took a break by going for a **walk in nature improved** their performance on an attention and memory task by **16%**. Students who went for a walk in an **urban environment did not improve** their scores.

2 Walking outside in the park **helped students all year round**. The season or weather made no difference.

3 Furthermore, those who walked in nature had a **positive boost** in their mood afterwards. Those who walked in urban environments didn't.

In the second study, they found that students who looked at photos of nature:

✔ **Performed better on memory and attention tests**

✔ **Had improved executive functioning**

✔ **Felt better and more refreshed afterwards**

Ref: Berman et al, 2008, *Psychological Science*

THE ONE ABOUT INTERACTING WITH NATURE

 ## RELATED RESEARCH

A recent study (#50) found that people who went on a short walk, even for just 5 minutes, had an increase in happiness, attentiveness and confidence. The participants in the study had the positive benefit of their walk regardless of whether they did it outside, in a gallery or on a treadmill.

This suggests that a walking break doesn't necessarily have to be done somewhere soothing, just that it shouldn't be somewhere stressful. As the authors of this study note, "unlike natural environments, urban environments are filled with stimulation that captures attention dramatically and additionally requires directed attention (e.g. to avoid being hit by a car), making them less restorative".

As well as walking, other research has studied simple day-to-day activities people can do to enhance memory, attention and well-being. These include getting a regular night's sleep (#29, #92), eating breakfast (#35) and drinking plenty of water. None of these strategies are particularly sophisticated or complicated. Perhaps that is the beauty of them: they have almost no cost, are easy to understand and can be actioned immediately. Furthermore, they almost instantly lead to tangible and meaningful change.

CLASSROOM IMPLICATIONS

The authors of this study start their write-up with a thought experiment: "Imagine a therapy that had no known side effects, was readily available and could improve your cognitive functioning at zero cost". Their results suggest that interacting with nature, either by going on a walk or looking at photos, does exactly this.

Students are often encouraged to take some breaks over the course of the day whilst they are revising. The results from this study suggest that not all breaks are equal. Doing so in a way that requires their brain to be alert is unlikely to have the desired effects. If we teach students about the advantages of taking a break in a manner that is both relaxing and refreshing, then they are more likely to not only feel better afterwards, but they are also more likely to remember more of their subsequent revision sessions.

THE ONE ABOUT STRESS AND UNCERTAINTY

@inner_drive | www.innerdrive.co.uk

THE STUDY

Researchers from University College London ran an experiment in which participants completed a learning game and received mild electric shocks that were delivered with varying predictability in order to stress them out.

The researchers wanted to find out **a)** the link between the feelings of uncertainty and of stress and **b)** if the two were linked, then what impact would there be on performance?

THE MAIN FINDINGS

1 Uncertainty is a **major cause** of how stressed people feel. This suggests that it is not the worst-case scenario that makes people really stressed, it is **the ambiguity of not knowing**.

2 Uncertainty **triggers** the major physiological **signatures of stress**, such as an increase in cortisol (the "stress hormone"), wider pupils and sweaty hands.

3 Some stress and uncertainty is actually **a good thing**, with participants in this condition doing better. This may be because it prompted them to **focus more and work harder**.

Ref: De Berker et al, 2016, *Nature Communications*

THE ONE ABOUT STRESS AND UNCERTAINTY

 ## RELATED RESEARCH

A growing body of research from both sport and education has examined the varying ways that people approach and reflect on a potentially stressful situation (#38). If people believe they have the skills and resources to meet the situation, feel in control of the event, surround themselves with supportive people and remember previous similar experiences, then they are more likely to view an event as a "challenge", whereas those who feel isolated focus on what they stand to lose if things go wrong, are overwhelmed by nerves, worry about looking bad and feel that their goals are unobtainable are more likely to be in a "threat state". People who view events as a challenge instead of a threat are more likely to manage their stress levels effectively.

In line with this thinking, a separate study found that someone's "stress mindset" can have a significant impact on performance (#51). Those that accepted that stress can sometimes be helpful were more likely to feel better, perform to a higher level and seek out more feedback during stressful situations. Furthermore, this stress mindset is malleable, meaning that people who learn about the potential benefits of stress can go on to cope with it more effectively.

CLASSROOM IMPLICATIONS

Certain situations are known to be more stressful for most students. These include exams, deadlines, public speaking and interviews. These events are seen as stressful, as they all have an element of uncertainty. The outcome is unsure and the consequences of both success and failure can have a significant impact on the lives and future choices that students make.

The findings from this study offer several practical suggestions for students. Firstly, understanding the triggers of stress (i.e. uncertainty) can help improve self-awareness of why students are feeling the way they are. Secondly, knowing that uncertainty - and, indeed, stress - can help enhance performance should be reassuring and help normalise these feelings. Thirdly, if students feel that their stress levels are excessively high and want to reduce them, then gathering information with the aim of reducing ambiguity and uncertainty will help.

THE ONE ABOUT METACOGNITION

@inner_drive | www.innerdrive.co.uk

THE STUDY

Metacognition refers to students' ability to monitor and direct their own learning effectively. It is seen as an essential part of developing independent learners. As such, it is a growing interest for researchers and teachers alike.

Researchers recently tested whether improving student metacognition, by having them answer simple study skills questions, would improve their academic achievements. They compared these students with a control group and then monitored how all the students studied for and performed during their exams.

THE MAIN FINDINGS

1 To **improve their metacognition**, students should reflect on **three questions**:

- Which resources do I need to help me study?
- Why are those resources helpful?
- How will I use this resource?

2 Asking these questions improved students' **self-reflection** and how **effective** they found their study resources when learning. They also felt **less stressed** and **more in control**.

3 These students went on to score **one-third of a grade higher** in their classes. They also did better on each exam. This was true for **all students**, regardless of their gender, age or academic ability.

Ref: Chen et al, 2017, Psychological Science

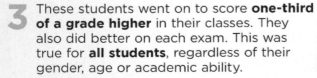

THE ONE ABOUT METACOGNITION

 ## RELATED RESEARCH

There is a growing body of evidence that suggests developing students' metacognitive skills leads to a boost in their motivation, learning and exam results (#84). Several studies have found that it is not just the quantity of studying they do, but the quality as well. Students who can effectively and efficiently use and manage the resources made available to them are the ones who tend to go on to achieve higher academic success.

Researchers from the Education Endowment Foundation in England suggest that this can add up to seven months of additional progress if implemented effectively. Encouragingly, several studies have found that metacognition is something that can be taught, learnt and developed. One such study found positive gains within two weeks of helping its students improve their metacognition.

Other studies have found that many students typically struggle to bridge the gap from having good intentions with actual behaviour change (#6). However, evidence suggests that those who do come up with specific action plans (as was the case in this study) do manage to do this better.

CLASSROOM IMPLICATIONS

Many schools now provide high-quality study resources for their students. However, the authors of this study note that:

> Regardless of how richly we endow students with study materials, support and environments conducive to learning, many of these resources will be wasted on students who do not thoughtfully use them in a productive manner. Encouraging students to be strategic in their use of class resources to master the class material enables them to leverage more of their potential during performance.

The researchers end their study on a positive note, when reflecting on the long-term benefit students will gain from developing their metacognitive abilities. They note that:

> Beyond education, there are many other situations in real life in which people engage in goal pursuit ineffectively . . . encouraging self-reflection in people about how to approach their goals strategically with the resources that are available to them can go a long way in helping them achieve their goals. This suggests that our students will continue to reap the rewards of improving metacognition long after their time in school has finished.

THE ONE ABOUT HELPING DISADVANTAGED STUDENTS

@inner_drive | www.innerdrive.co.uk

THE STUDY

The Programme for International Student Assessment (PISA) is the largest worldwide study on how students from around the world are progressing. It is released every three years and reports on data from over half a million students from over 50 countries.

Recently, researchers analysed the mountains of data to examine which countries are good at helping their disadvantaged students succeed in maths, reading and science. They also examined which countries have got better at this over the past decade and what characteristics their schools share that help these students flourish.

THE MAIN FINDINGS

1 The countries that had the **highest percentage of disadvantaged** students performing well at school were China, Singapore, Estonia, Japan and Finland.

2 The countries that **had improved** in this area the most in the last ten years included Portugal, Germany, Norway, Israel, Slovenia and Spain.

3 **Factors associated** with **helping disadvantaged** students develop academic resilience and perform better included attending schools with:

  ✔ A good disciplinary classroom climate
  ✔ A range of extra-curricular activities
  ✔ High attendance rates
  ✔ More affluent pupils

4 Factors that were **not associated** with **helping disadvantaged** students included classroom facilities (i.e. computers) and smaller classroom sizes.

Ref: Agasisti et al, 2018, *OECD Education Working Papers*

THE ONE ABOUT HELPING DISADVANTAGED STUDENTS

RELATED RESEARCH

This study highlights the benefit of having a clear and orderly classroom structure. A fascinating area of research has investigated how to achieve this. Evidence suggests that schools that have a low turnover of teachers have a better disciplinary climate in their classrooms. Research suggests that teacher turnover can be reduced by developing mentoring programmes for staff within the school, encouraging collaboration between staff and helping new staff feel a sense of belonging towards the school.

Another factor associated with classroom culture and disciplinary climate is the leadership style of the principals at this school. Termed "transformational leadership", this is characterised by emphasising staff development, encouraging staff to have high expectations of their students and creating orderly classrooms. Somewhat ominously, the authors of the research note that "the managerial skills that enable principals to develop and effectively implement a transformational leadership style in their schools are seldom taught in academic programmes that train school principals".

CLASSROOM IMPLICATIONS

The authors of this study note that "school policies and practices can affect the probability of disadvantaged students to obtain good academic results, meaning that student resilience is not only determined by their background and home resources, but also by the schools they attend". Specifically, they highlight one particular aspect of importance when they note that "attending orderly classes in which students can focus and teachers provide well-placed instruction is beneficial for all students, but particularly so for the most vulnerable students".

This study also suggests that it is not having the nicest or the largest number of facilities that drives improvement, but rather it is the experiences, activities and culture that are more important. This is reassuring to know, as it means that interventions need not be expensive or based on the latest technology. Rather it is about providing opportunities and having a clear vision, values and behavioural policies in place.

THE ONE ABOUT PICTURING THE PROCESS

@inner_drive | www.innerdrive.co.uk

THE STUDY

It is one week before an exam. Is it better to visualise yourself studying for the exam or is it better to visualise what life would be like if you did well in the exam? Researchers ran a study with 101 students to find out.

In this study, some of the students were instructed to picture themselves revising, whereas others were told to imagine finding out that they had achieved a high grade on the test. The researchers then recorded how the students felt in the build-up to the exam, how much revision they did and, finally, what grade they got.

THE MAIN FINDINGS

1 One week before the exam, students who spent **just a few minutes visualising themselves studying**, instead of seeing themselves doing well in the test, reported that they:

✔ **Had a clearer plan of what they needed to do**

✔ **Felt less nervous about the exam**

✔ **Were going to spend more time studying**

✔ **Expected to do better in the exam**

2 The day after the exam, the researchers found out that students **who had visualised themselves studying,** instead of **doing well in the test:**

✔ Did **40%** more revision in the final week

✔ Got over **8%** higher marks in their exam

✔ **Outperformed the class average by some distance, whereas those who visualised their desired outcome did worse**

Ref: Pham and Taylor, 1999, *Personality and Social Psychology Bulletin*

THE ONE ABOUT PICTURING THE PROCESS

RELATED RESEARCH

Previous research on visualisation has found that it can be particularly helpful in enhancing emotions, which in turn are linked with academic success (#58). However, and in support of this study, other research has found a darker side to visualisation. A rather fascinating and quirky study found that for participants who were trying to lose weight, if they visualised the outcome, - such as the amount of weight they wanted to lose - they were more likely to be tempted by the offer of free doughnuts. Focusing too much on the outcome can have a detrimental effect.

Within education, other studies have found that students who spent time imagining that their week was going to be great actually reported being less energised and achieved less over the seven days than those in a control group. Likewise, similar results were found in students who spent time visualising their perfect job. Upon graduation, these students received fewer job offers and had a lower starting wage than those who did not do this type of visualisation.

CLASSROOM IMPLICATIONS

This study gives an indication of how we can best help students both prepare for upcoming exams and manage their emotions whilst doing so. Helping them focus on the behaviours they need to have in order to succeed will ensure that they are more likely to complete the right actions. Focusing too much on the outcome may further exacerbate procrastination and daydreaming, as well as enhancing anxiety about the exam by focusing too much on the destination and not the journey itself. Essentially, "a student who wishes to become a surgeon would improve his or her chances by mentally stimulating the steps he or she must go through to achieve that goal rather than envisioning him or herself in the desired end state".

The authors of the study conclude with a famous, albeit anonymous, quote: "the will to win is not nearly as important as the will to prepare to win". They state that instead of having an "I can do it" attitude, students would be better placed having a "how can I do it?" one instead.

THE ONE ABOUT WHAT TEACHERS SAY

@inner_drive | www.innerdrive.co.uk

THE STUDY

How much does the type and frequency of communication used by a teacher have an impact on their students? Do the throwaway comments resonate long after they have been said? And do these comments affect students in different ways based on either the subject they are being taught or the type of student?

To find out, this study recorded young students' perceptions of how their teacher talked to them and measured this against how the students talked to themselves, how they viewed themselves and how well they did at school.

THE MAIN FINDINGS

1 Frequent positive statements by teachers were found to be:

- ✓ Directly related to student positive self-talk

- ✓ Directly related to maths performance

- ✓ Directly related to whether students viewed themselves as good learners

- ✓ Indirectly related to students' reading self-concept

2 Frequent negative statements by teachers were found to be:

- ✓ Predictive of how girls viewed themselves as mathematicians

- ✓ Directly related to the amount of negative self-talk boys had

Ref: Burnett, 1999, *Educational Psychology in Practice*

THE ONE ABOUT WHAT TEACHERS SAY

RELATED RESEARCH

A whole host of research has found a link between how parents and teachers talk to students and how students talk to themselves. Generally speaking, these studies have found that positive interactions result in students viewing themselves in a better light (#9). Likewise, negative interactions often lead to a negative self-perception (#7). Furthermore, these effects appear to be long-lasting, with these consequences and beliefs being held firmly for many years after the initial comments have been made.

It is interesting to note that in this study, boys and girls reacted differently to a teacher's negative self-talk but in similar ways to their teacher's positive self-talk. The research on this difference is still in its early stages and more work is needed before firm conclusions can be drawn.

CLASSROOM IMPLICATIONS

The challenge facing teachers here is that students sometimes struggle to separate feedback on the task with feedback on who they are as a person. Therefore, feedback offering a critique on a particular piece of work may be interpreted as a personal attack. This means that a) we need to help educate students on how to receive feedback better and b) be very careful with our words, as both positive and negative statements made by teachers can have a significant impact on students.

How students talk to themselves is of great importance, given that other research has associated positive and helpful self-talk with mindset, resilience, self-esteem, creativity, concentration and motivation. In terms of self-talk, research is starting to move away from the positive vs negative dichotomy. This is because, if framed correctly, negative self-talk can help spur on future efforts. Instead, research is focusing more on helpful versus unhelpful self-talk. This offers a more constructive and productive way of viewing self-talk.

THE ONE ABOUT PARENTAL WARMTH

@inner_drive | www.innerdrive.co.uk

THE STUDY

Researchers recently investigated how much weight the type and frequency of communication that parents have with their children impacts on their child's development. To find out, they tracked 565 children and their parents over a two-year period. During that time, both parents and children were regularly surveyed to find out how the parents felt they communicated with their children, how the children perceived this communication and what the consequences of it were.

The researchers specifically looked at parental over-praising ("my child is more special than other children"), parental warmth ("I let my child know I love him/her"), the children's self-esteem ("kids like me are happy with themselves as a person") and narcissism ("kids like me deserve something extra").

THE MAIN FINDINGS

1 The **consequences** of parents **over-praising** included:

✔ **Children displaying more narcissistic behaviours**

✔ **No difference in their child's self-esteem levels**

2 **Parental warmth** led to:

✔ **Children having higher levels of self-esteem**

✔ **Did not make the children more narcissistic**

They concluded that "parent-training interventions might be one effective means to curtail narcissistic development. Such interventions can help parents convey affection and appreciation to children without conveying to children that they are superior to others".

Ref: Brummelman et al, 2015, *Proceedings of the National Academy of Sciences*

THE ONE ABOUT PARENTAL WARMTH

 ## RELATED RESEARCH

The area of narcissism has fascinated people ever since the mythological Greek figure Narcissus exclaimed that "the spark I kindle is the torch I carry". Researchers have distinguished narcissism with self-esteem by describing the former as "passionately wanting to think well of oneself" and the latter as actually "thinking well of oneself". Self-esteem has been associated with lower levels of anxiety and depression, whereas narcissism has been associated with stress, feelings of humiliation and a range of mental health problems.

In the quest to promote high self-esteem in children, many parents were previously advised to lavishly praise them to reinforce all the good things they were doing. Unfortunately, not only has lavish praise been found to be associated with lowering expectations, but this study suggests that it does not boost self-esteem and that it actually drives the exact type of narcissistic behaviours we want to avoid.

Likewise, other evidence (#19) suggests that the type of praise children hear when they are as young as 1 year old can predict their mindset up to five years later, with those that receive comments about their natural abilities and achievements being more likely to develop a fixed mindset compared to those who had heard praise about their behaviour, effort and strategy.

CLASSROOM IMPLICATIONS

The authors of the study note that "children come to see themselves as they believe to be seen by significant others, as if they learn to see themselves through other eyes" and that:

> When children are seen by their parents as being more special and more entitled than other children, they may internalize the view that they are superior individuals, a view that is at the core of narcissism. However, when children are treated by their parents with affection and appreciation, they may internalize the view that they are valuable individuals, a view that is at the core of self-esteem.

THE ONE ABOUT HOW MUCH WE FORGET

@inner_drive | www.innerdrive.co.uk

THE STUDY

In 1880, German psychologist Hermann Ebbinghaus conducted one of the most famous studies ever. He wanted to see how quickly people forget things over time. He was the first to try to find a mathematical equation that describes that shape of forgetting. The result, called "the forgetting curve" is often presented something like this:

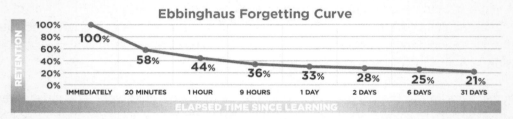

Ebbinghaus Forgetting Curve

RETENTION

100%
80%
60%
40%
20%
0%

100% — IMMEDIATELY
58% — 20 MINUTES
44% — 1 HOUR
36% — 9 HOURS
33% — 1 DAY
28% — 2 DAYS
25% — 6 DAYS
21% — 31 DAYS

ELAPSED TIME SINCE LEARNING

Over 130 years later, researchers from The University of Amsterdam sought to replicate and update his findings using modern statistical analysis and experimental procedures.

THE MAIN FINDINGS

1 Generally speaking, Ebbinghaus' findings were replicated – people suffer **a drop in memory soon after the event**, with this decline then slowing down over time.

2 However, they found that people receive **a boost to memory** after 24 hours, with their participants remembering **more in the morning** of the second day than they did in the night of the first. This jump is due to the negative impact fatigue has on memory and the power that sleep has to combat this.

3 People tend to remember **the first** and **the last things** they learn more than the things in the middle. These are called the **primacy and recency effects**, respectively.

4 The researchers advised that "the forgetting curve" is **not set in stone**. Instead, it is better to see it as **a guide**.

Ref: Murre and Dros, 2015, *PLoS ONE*

THE ONE ABOUT HOW MUCH WE FORGET

 ## RELATED RESEARCH

A growing number of studies in cognitive, educational and developmental psychology have struggled to have their initial findings replicated. That is what makes studies like this so valuable. The authors of the study conclude with praise for Ebbinghaus by saying that he:

> Set new standards for psychology experiments, already incorporating such 'modern' concepts as controlled stimulus, counter-balancing of time of day effects, guarding against optional stopping, statistical data analysis and modelling to find a concise mathematical description and further verify his results. The result was a high-quality forgetting curve that has rightfully remained a classic in the field. Replications, including ours, testify to the soundness of his results.

In the last few decades, researchers have built on this classic study by examining the amount of information that students forget over the summer holidays (#94) and the role of "spacing out learning" (#4). They have found that as people often forget information quickly, it is important to revisit it. It is this very act of forgetting and re-learning that actually cements knowledge into our long-term memory. Essentially, doing one hour a day for seven days is more effective than doing seven hours in one day, as the latter will fall short because of the nature of Ebbinghaus's forgetting curve.

CLASSROOM IMPLICATIONS

This area of study has powerful implications for how our students learn. With modular exams becoming increasingly rare, the challenge now is how to best teach a large amount of material over the course of two years without students forgetting it. Clearly, doing module one followed by module two and then module three and so on will be less effective, as by the time they get to module 20, module one will have all but been forgotten. Therefore, it makes sense to consistently and regularly refer back to previous work and to revisit prior material.

The best way to think about this is as follows: just because something has been taught, does not mean it has been deeply learnt. Topics must be revisited and retaught. Only by doing this can we help students overcome the forgetting curve and maximise their learning.

THE ONE ABOUT HOMEWORK

@inner_drive | www.innerdrive.co.uk

THE STUDY

How regularly should teachers set homework? Does the amount of time students spend on their homework make any difference? And should they struggle on their own or do it with the support of their parents? Researchers investigated these questions by looking at 7,451 teenagers from Spain, with an average age of just under 14 years.

THE MAIN FINDINGS

1 Students who were set **regular homework** by their teacher performed **significantly better** than those who were only set it occasionally.

2 The frequency that homework was set was found to be **more important** than the **amount of time** students spent on it.

3 Students who spent **90–110 minutes a day** doing homework **got the highest** scores.

4 Researchers found that although 90–110 minutes was the **most effective**, it was not the most efficient as the **extra time spent** after one hour led to minimal gains that **did not justify** the extra time.

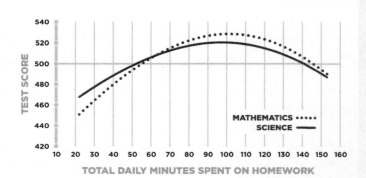

Chart — TEST SCORE (420–540) vs TOTAL DAILY MINUTES SPENT ON HOMEWORK (10–160)

MATHEMATICS ●●●●●
SCIENCE ———

5 Students who did their homework **by themselves** ended up doing around **10% better** in their exams than those who did their homework with their parents helping them.

Good job!

Ref: Fernandez-Alonso et al, 2015, *Journal of Educational Psychology*

THE ONE ABOUT HOMEWORK

 ## RELATED RESEARCH

Most of the research to date has found a positive relationship between homework and academic achievement. These include studies from Great Britain, Germany, Holland and Switzerland. Although not all studies are so conclusive, what is certainly clear is that it is not linear; more does not always equal better.

This study adds to that research by taking a more nuanced approach by looking at frequency, duration and if students do it independently. Doing homework independently encourages autonomy, which has been linked with developing self-regulation. Other research to date has found that it is not just the frequency of homework that teachers set, but the quality of it.

Finally, the age of the students and the benefits of homework have also been investigated. For students in secondary school, the relationship between homework and grades is a positive one. However, this is not the case for primary school students, with homework having a limited positive impact.

CLASSROOM IMPLICATIONS

The researchers of this study emphasise that:

> Our data sends a clear message to teaching professionals: well used, homework remains a vital tool for comprehensive education of adolescents . . . it is not necessary to assign huge quantities of homework, but it is important that assignment is systematic and regular, with the aim of instilling work habits and promoting autonomous, self-directed learning. Homework should not exclusively aim for repetition of content, as this type of task is associated with less effort or lower results . . . the conclusion is that when it comes to homework how is more important than how much.

These findings are important given that a) teachers spend a lot of time setting and marking homework and b) some students spend an excessive amount of time doing the homework. This study suggests that we can reduce workload and improve student performance by setting the right amount and right type of homework.

THE ONE ABOUT MINDSET, ATTITUDE AND SELF-ESTEEM

@inner_drive | www.innerdrive.co.uk

THE STUDY

Previous research has found that when performing an experiment in a laboratory, students who feel that they have a growth mindset (i.e. the belief they can improve) think more productively and perform better in subsequent tasks than those who have a fixed mindset (i.e. the belief that their ability is set in stone). But does this translate into the real world?

Researchers tracked over 500 students over the course of their four years at university to find out if having a growth or fixed mindset impacted how they thought, felt and behaved. This included how they explained their successes, failures and changes to their self-esteem.

THE MAIN FINDINGS

1 Those with a growth mindset were more likely to:

- ▸ **Prioritise learning goals over performance ones**
- ▸ **Attribute their success to their efforts and study skills**
- ▸ **Feel excited, inspired and enthusiastic about their academic performance**
- ▸ **Put in more effort or learn from their mistakes in the face of adversity**
- ▸ **Have an increase in self-esteem during late adolescence**

2 Those with a fixed mindset were more likely to:

- ▸ **Prioritise immediate performance over learning**
- ▸ **Attribute both their failures and successes to external and uncontrollable factors, such as luck**
- ▸ **Feel distressed, ashamed and upset about their academic performance**
- ▸ **Give up and feel helpless in the face of adversity**
- ▸ **Suffer a dip in self-esteem during late adolescence**

Ref: Robins and Pals, 2002, *Self and Identity*

THE ONE ABOUT MINDSET, ATTITUDE AND SELF-ESTEEM

RELATED RESEARCH

This research supports and builds on previous findings that highlight the different behaviours and thought processes of those with a growth or fixed mindset (#5, #14). It is encouraging to see research moving beyond the laboratory and being tested in real-world situations.

One interesting area of study has found that helping students realise that their personality is not fixed has helped reduce anxiety and depression symptoms. Likewise, helping students adapt their mindset towards stress - that is, helping them realise that stress is not always a bad thing - has helped improve student performance in the face of adversity (#51).

The findings in this study - that those with a growth mindset are more likely to adopt learning instead of performance goals - is interesting. Other research has found that those who adopt a learning orientation are more likely to spend longer on the task, work harder, display more resilience, choose challenging tasks and have more pride and satisfaction in their work.

CLASSROOM IMPLICATIONS

This study highlights that how we view ourselves can impact how we explain both our successes and failures, our self-esteem and indeed our future goals. Beyond just academic grades, it suggests that the growth mindset theory can fundamentally shape how students view their educational experience and alters their perception of how much control they have over it.

The researchers state that those with a fixed mindset:

> Explain academic achievement - both successes and failures - in terms of external factors . . . thus they are truly helpless and assume that both their successes and failures are out of their control. In a sense, they are caught in a trap: they strive for academic success to prove their high ability, yet they explain away their successes as due to luck.

On the other hand, those with a growth mindset "believe they just need to try harder or use better study strategies to perform better". Helping guide our students towards having a growth mindset offers a promising strategy to help them better navigate their school life.

THE ONE ABOUT PRE-QUESTIONS

@inner_drive | www.innerdrive.co.uk

THE STUDY

It is common practice to ask students questions at the end of a lesson or during their revision session in order to check to see how much they have learnt. But does it help boost their memory to ask them questions about the material before they have actually learnt it? The effectiveness of this technique, referred to as "Pre-Questioning", was recently tested by researchers from Iowa State University.

They divided students into two groups. Some received pre-questions about the material they were about to learn from a video clip. The others just watched the video clip. They were all then tested to see how much they remembered.

THE MAIN FINDINGS

1 Students **who had been given pre-questions** did **much better** in the test than those who didn't.

2 This benefit was not contained to topics that had been pre-questioned. Students **in the pre-question group** also did **24% better** than their peers on questions on topics on which they had not been pre-questioned.

Ref: Carpenter and Toftness, 2017, *Journal of Applied Research in Memory and Cognition*

THE ONE ABOUT PRE-QUESTIONS

RELATED RESEARCH

Research into pre-questions has found that they can be effective regardless of whether they are multiple choice, open ended, fill-in-the-blank or short-answer questions. Researchers have offered three possible reasons as to why they may be effective. Firstly, that the use of pre-questions allows students to preview the nature of the lesson. Secondly, it arouses a sense of curiosity and engagement. Thirdly, and finally, it can help reduce overconfidence in learners who may approach a lesson believing they already know everything. This then makes them more responsive to the lesson and open to learning.

However, a word of warning is needed. There is evidence to suggest that when students are given pre-questions before a self-paced reading task, it can actually hinder learning. Why might this be the case? The researchers note that:

> Pre-questions might encourage the selective processing of information during reading, in that participants attend more strongly to the information in the passage that is most relevant to the pre-questions and attend less to (or possibly skip altogether) information that is not relevant to the pre-questions.

CLASSROOM IMPLICATIONS

The authors acknowledge that their results may sound counterintuitive to educators as "how can students answer a question about material they have not yet learned?" but do stress that "research shows that pre-questions can significantly enhance students' encoding, and later memory, of the to-be-learned information". It is therefore worth considering how to best start a lesson. Instead of learning objectives or lesson outcomes, pre-questions may offer a better way to begin things.

As mentioned earlier, there is a potential downside to pre-questions if the teacher does not control the pace of the lesson (i.e. in self-directed reading tasks). Therefore, this technique is best utilised in lessons where information is presented by video or PowerPoint. Research is still ongoing into how long the memory boost of pre-questions lasts, so it is probably best to use it as an opener to boost curiosity for lessons and also in conjunction with other proven memory strategies such as retrieval practice (#23), spacing (#4) and interleaving (#15).

THE ONE ABOUT THE LEARNING STYLE MYTH

@inner_drive | www.innerdrive.co.uk

THE STUDY

The learning style theory states that we each have a "learning style" such as "visual", "auditory" or "kinaesthetic". Further, pupils who are taught in a way that complements their "learning style" will learn and perform better. But is there any evidence to back up this theory?

Four professors of psychology in the United States performed a thorough review of all the research available to see if the claims made by proponents of the learning style theory stacked up.

THE MAIN FINDINGS

1 **Preferences, not styles:** Students may have a preference for the way that they want to learn. However, this is not the same as having a learning style. A preference is **what you like the most,** not necessarily the way you would learn best.

2 **Absence of positive findings:** The researchers could not find a single study where teaching someone in their "learning style" led to them getting better results.

3 **Evidence of negative findings:** There is however a significant amount of evidence that students who were taught in their favourite style did no better. This was found to be true in a wide range of settings, including education, medicine and in psychology laboratories.

4 **Decide how to teach the content based on what is being taught.** For example, the researchers noted that "the optimal curriculum for a writing course probably includes a heavy verbal emphasis, whereas the most efficient and effective model of teaching geometry obviously requires visual-spatial materials".

5 Even **if research found a positive impact** of teaching students according to their styles (which it hasn't), the impact **would have to be very large** to justify the time, energy and cost of doing it.

Ref: Pashler et al, 2008, *Psychological Science in the Public Interest*

THE ONE ABOUT THE LEARNING STYLE MYTH

RELATED RESEARCH

A survey in 2012 found that the learning style myth is still prevalent in schools, with 93% of UK teachers believing it. It is quite difficult to discuss the related research in this area, as it is marked by a notable absence of any research into the efficacy of the application of the "learning styles theory". This was the core finding of this research paper.

However, one other study is worth noting, which found that teaching students using a range and combination of senses will often lead to better learning as it will help keep their attention and will help embed the content more in their long-term memory. This suggests that not only is just teaching someone to their learning style less effective but also that it can actually limit how much students learn.

CLASSROOM IMPLICATIONS

Why have learning styles become so popular in education? Apart from the desire to categorise people, the authors of the study note that:

> If a person or person's child is not succeeding or excelling school, it may be more comfortable for the person to think that the educational system, not the person or the child himself or herself, is responsible. That is, rather than attribute one's lack of success to any lack of ability or effort on one's part, it may be more appealing to think that the fault lies with instruction being inadequately tailored to one's learning style.

The researchers conclude their paper with a call to arms to those in education, by stating that:

> If education is to be transformed into an evidence-based field, it is important not only to identify teaching techniques that have experimental support but also to identify which widely held beliefs affect the choices made by educational practitioners but lack empirical support.

They also state the following:

> That at present, there is no adequate evidence base to justify incorporating learning-styles assessment into general educational practice. Thus, limited education resources would be better devoted to adopting other educational practices that have a strong evidence base, of which there are a number.

THE ONE ABOUT EATING DINNER TOGETHER

@inner_drive | www.innerdrive.co.uk

THE STUDY

Families are now far less likely to eat meals together regularly than they were in the past. But what impact does regular family meal times have on student development? To find out, researchers surveyed almost 100,000 students from over 213 cities.

THE MAIN FINDINGS

1 More than half of young teenagers ate dinner with their family 5–7 times a week. This number **dropped to just over a third** for older teenagers.

2 Children who regularly ate dinner with their family **reported enhanced**:

- ✔ **Communication with their parents**
- ✔ **Parental involvement in school**
- ✔ **Motivation levels**
- ✔ **School engagement and time spent on homework**
- ✔ **Self-esteem**
- ✔ **Ability to plan and make decisions**
- ✔ **Optimism about their future**

3 Children who regularly ate dinner with their family **reported less**:

- ✔ **Alcohol use**
- ✔ **Tobacco use**
- ✔ **Drug use**
- ✔ **Depressive symptoms**
- ✔ **Anti-social behaviour**
- ✔ **Violent tendencies**
- ✔ **Problems at school**

Ref: Fulker et al, 2006, *Journal of Adolescent Health*

THE ONE ABOUT EATING DINNER TOGETHER

 ## RELATED RESEARCH

Other research has focused not only on frequency of family mealtimes, but what families do during those times. One such study found that one-third of children report watching television whilst eating with their parents. This was associated with them eating fewer vegetables, drinking more fizzy drinks and consuming more fats. However, it is worth noting that these children still had a healthier diet than those who did not eat regularly with their family.

Eating dinner as a family has also been shown to help teenagers create dietary habits that stick with them into adulthood. This chimes with other research that found similar effects for eating breakfast regularly as a child. Evidence suggests that eating dinner as a family and eating breakfast regularly as a child have decreased over the past 30 years, but that by planning what to eat and scheduling time together to do so, families can change this.

CLASSROOM IMPLICATIONS

Although this study looked at correlation and not causation, the authors do suggest that "adolescents may learn social skills and develop a more positive self-worth during mealtime interactions". This raises three interesting thoughts. Firstly, what happens to students who do not experience regular mealtimes? Does this go some way into helping us understand both them as an individual as well as their daily lives?

Secondly, how can we best help those students who do not experience eating with others? A growing feature in many schools recently has been the use of nurture rooms, which aim to replicate this type of experience so that students can practice developing relationships. Thirdly and finally, it also highlights the need to emphasise to parents the importance of eating together as a family. This is difficult for parents, many of whom are either working late hours or on shift work, but nudging parents to take as many opportunities as they can to eat with their children likely will lead to a boost in both student character and academic performance.

THE ONE ABOUT ELECTRONIC NOTE-TAKING

@inner_drive | www.innerdrive.co.uk

THE STUDY

Technology is playing an ever-increasing role in education. It is now common to see students taking notes using electronic devices, be it laptops or tablets. But which is better for note-taking; pen and paper, or electronics?

Researchers investigated how students differed in the type of notes they took depending on the device they used, how well they could subsequently apply the knowledge learnt during their lesson and how well they did on their final exams.

THE MAIN FINDINGS

1 Those who took notes with a laptop **performed worse** when they had to answer conceptual-application questions.

2 Those who took notes on their laptops wrote up to **30% more words** than those who did so on paper. They were also more likely to take notes verbatim. Taking notes verbatim **leads to shallower learning** as it does not require the student to think about what they are typing.

3 Even if the lecturers told students about **the cost** of taking notes down word for word on the laptop, this had no impact. They **still did** so.

4 Students were given the chance to review their notes before the final exam. Those **who took notes using pen and paper outperformed** those who took notes on their laptop.

Ref: Mueller and Oppenheimer, 2014, *Psychological Science*

THE ONE ABOUT ELECTRONIC NOTE-TAKING

 ## RELATED RESEARCH

A recent study has failed to replicate some of the findings in this study. However, the jury is still out, and it is worth noting that several other studies have found that students who take notes on laptops struggle to stay on task, as they succumb to the numerous online temptations such as streaming videos, social networking and shopping.

The type of notes that students take with their laptops makes a difference. Students have been found to be more likely to take notes verbatim, as they can type faster than they can write. However, several studies have confirmed that doing so leads to less cognitive processing and as such, less information is retained. The researchers of this study offer another suggestion as to why students who took notes by hand performed better, commenting that, as students had to go slower, they were forced to select "more important information to include in their notes, which enables them to study the content more efficiently".

CLASSROOM IMPLICATIONS

The authors conclude with a clear word of warning over the use of laptops for note-taking when they say that "laptop use can negatively affect performance on educational assessments, even – or perhaps especially – when they computer is used for its intended function of easier note taking". Essentially, students shouldn't strive to make taking notes too easy, as this reduces the opportunity for deep reflection and learning. Or as the authors say, there is real value in having "desirable difficulty".

This is not to say that laptops can't provide some unique learning opportunities, such as access to wider information quickly, but that there is an opportunity cost. The best way to view them is with "a healthy dose of caution; despite their growing popularity, laptops may be doing more harm in classrooms than good".

THE ONE ABOUT THE BANDWAGON EFFECT

@inner_drive | www.innerdrive.co.uk

THE STUDY

Do students know their own mind or are they likely to follow the crowd? What if they think the crowd is doing the wrong thing, will they still go along with them? This is known as the bandwagon effect, which describes the likelihood of people of doing something because everyone else is.

Groups of students were asked to publicly state how long they thought a line was. Unbeknownst to the real participant, everyone else in the room was an actor and were all under instructions to give false answers. Would the real participant give the correct answer or follow the group and get it wrong?

THE MAIN FINDINGS

1 In about a **third of the experiments**, participants **followed the group** and gave a wrong answer.

2 When in the presence of others, **75%** **gave a wrong answer** at least once.

3 When they were **on their own**, people stated the **correct answer** more than **99%** of the time.

4 In interviews afterwards, **participants who followed the group** and got it wrong said they did so either because of **low confidence**, they thought the group knew best, or they suspected everyone else was wrong but had a desire to conform and fit in.

Ref: Asch, 1951, Groups, *Leadership and Men*

THE ONE ABOUT THE BANDWAGON EFFECT

RELATED RESEARCH

Following on from his original research, Solomon Asch investigated under which conditions people are most likely to conform. He found that the number of other people stating the wrong answer had an impact: only one person stating a false answer led to an error rate of 3%, two people stating a false answer increased the error rate to 13% and three people stating a false answer resulted in in an error rate of 32%. Increasing this beyond three people did not appear to alter conformity levels.

More recent studies have found that the bandwagon effect occurs in situations beyond the psych lab. For example, one such study found that hotel guests were more likely to reuse their towels (and thus save the hotel laundry costs) if they believed that the other guests in the hotel were also doing so.

The impact that other people have on decision making has been extensively studied in adolescents. It is interesting to note how most risky decisions - for example, smoking, underage drinking and speeding whilst driving - happen in the presence of others. This suggests that we are all prone to the bandwagon effect, but that teenagers are especially so (#8).

CLASSROOM IMPLICATIONS

This line of research has interesting implications for teachers on two separate levels. Firstly, is that it is easy to get into a state of "group-think", which is when people fail to critically evaluate the quality of a suggestion because many other people say it is good. This is how and why fads and neuro-myths creep into education and mainstream consciousness.

Secondly, the bandwagon effect explains why students may think and behave differently when part of a group than they do when they are on their own. In this study, some participants reported knowing that the answer they were giving was wrong but did so anyway because of social pressure. Helping students know their own mind and not make bad decisions "just because everyone else is" may prove to be one of the more valuable skills needed to navigate the tricky teenage years.

THE ONE ABOUT STRUGGLING SCIENTISTS

@inner_drive | www.innerdrive.co.uk

THE STUDY

Researchers investigated what impact, if any, hearing about the life and struggles of successful scientists had on students' grades. In their study, they divided the students into three groups. Each heard different details about Albert Einstein, Marie Curie and Michael Faraday. Some were told about the struggles in their career, such as failed experiments, and how they overcame them with persistence. Others were told about the struggles in their personal life such as poverty and lack of parental support. Finally, others were just told about their greatest achievements.

THE MAIN FINDINGS

1 Hearing about **successful scientists who struggled,** either in their personal or professional lives, helped students feel more connected to them.

This led to these students going on to **achieve better grades** than those who had just heard about their greatest achievement.

2 This effect was most pronounced in students who **were currently struggling academically** in their science lessons.

3 Students who had only heard about the famous scientists who had achieved a lot in their career, **had a decline** in grades.

This was attributed to them feeling **less connected** to them and believing they would never have as high scientific abilities in comparison.

The authors conclude their study by stating that "students' beliefs that success in science depends on exceptional talent, negatively impacts their motivation to learn". However, they go on to finish with a more upbeat and positive note by suggesting that teaching students about how others have had to overcome struggles on their way to success "can be implemented in classrooms to improve motivation and learning in science, and likely other subjects as well".

Ref: Lin-Siegler et al, 2016, *Journal of Educational Psychology*

THE ONE ABOUT STRUGGLING SCIENTISTS

RELATED RESEARCH

If students attribute their failures to stable and internal factors, such as a perceived lack of intelligence, then this can lead to a self-fulfilling prophecy in which lack of effort leads to failure. This can be very stressful and demotivating, as they believe that there is little they can do to affect their outcome.

Research has shown that to overcome this learned helplessness, people could try attributing their failures to temporary factors, such as luck or effort. This will lead to higher levels of both optimism and performance.

CLASSROOM IMPLICATIONS

If students believe that exceptional ability and high intelligence are a pre-requisite for success in science and maths courses then fewer students will choose to study these subjects, and will feel threatened by those who are doing well and will give up quicker when setbacks occur. In essence, "when students struggle in science class, they may misperceive their struggle as an indication that they are not good at science and will never succeed in it".

Helping students reframe their perception of what it takes to succeed using stories has been found to a very effective medium. The authors state that this is because "stories are memorable because people become emotionally involved in the lives of the characters, see the world as they do, or imagine situations that may be similar to theirs".

Many scientific textbooks contain details about some of the greatest scientific findings, such as Einstein's general theory of relativity, Marie Curie's use of radium to treat cancer and Michael Faraday's work on electromagnetism. This study suggests that only hearing about these may demotivate some struggling students who feel inferior in comparison. If students are also told the story behind these achievements, especially the resilience and persistence needed, it will capture their attention and boost their performance.

THE ONE ABOUT EFFECTIVE TEACHERS

@inner_drive | www.innerdrive.co.uk

THE STUDY

What predicts how effective a teacher is? For young teachers entering the classroom for the first time, the thought of teaching a large group of students can be a daunting affair. But what are the key personality traits that help separate the best from the rest?

A team of researchers tracked 390 novice teachers who were teaching in challenging schools and measured student grades over the course of the year against the personality traits of their teachers.

THE MAIN FINDINGS

1 Student grades **significantly increased** if their teacher had:

✓ Passion and persistence for their job (often known in research as "grit").

✓ High levels of life satisfaction – the authors note that "teachers higher in life satisfaction may be more adept at engaging their pupils, and their zest and enthusiasm may spread to their students".

✓ Optimism and the ability to bounce back from setbacks.

2 Teachers who taught in primary schools or to students with special educational needs **had the most impact**.

Ref: Duckworth et al, 2009, *Journal of Positive Psychology*

THE ONE ABOUT EFFECTIVE TEACHERS

RELATED RESEARCH

Much research has been conducted on what makes a good teacher (#21, #79). One such area is experience, with one large-scale review finding that the more experienced a teacher is, the more their students learnt. It is worth noting, that large gains in this area were found in the early years of one's teaching career.

Somewhat counterintuitively, evidence suggests that the education level of a teacher does not predict student outcome. This may be because having a good knowledge of a particular topic does not always translate into being able to teach that knowledge effectively.

Research away from education has found that "in prior studies, grittier individuals work harder and longer in very challenging settings than did their less gritty peers". Likewise, other studies that examine teacher stress levels have found that a teacher's mood and well-being is transferred to their students. These studies combine to provide supporting evidence for this study, which found that resilient teachers who have high life satisfaction help their students make additional progress.

CLASSROOM IMPLICATIONS

More and more teachers are leaving the classroom each year and fewer and fewer are being recruited, especially for subjects such as maths, science and English. Though it may be too early to draw firm conclusions, studies like this may be able to help guide schools on who best to appoint and how best to support those already in place.

This study ends on a positive note by stating that although relatively stable, evidence indicates that the three factors studied here (grit, life satisfaction and optimism) are malleable and as such, may be good areas to target as part of teacher training and ongoing CPD. As the authors note, "given the crucial role played by teachers in the lives and learning of children, the possibility of improving their capabilities seems worth testing".

THE ONE ABOUT RETRIEVAL PRACTICE AND STRESS

@inner_drive | www.innerdrive.co.uk

THE STUDY

Are students who revise using retrieval practice better able to recall that information when they are stressed, such as in highly pressurised exams? To find out, researchers had half their students revise by doing lots of tests and quizzes (i.e. retrieval practice) and the other half revise by re-reading key passages of the text. They then placed half of each group in either stressful or non-stressful environments and recorded how much they were able to remember.

THE MAIN FINDINGS

1 Those who revised **using retrieval practice outperformed** those who had just re-read their notes by **17–26%**

2 Increased stress made those who **studied by re-reading** their notes perform up to **32%** worse.

3 Increased stress **did not negatively affect** the memory of those who used **retrieval practice**.

4 Retrieval practice **was so effective** at combating the negative effect of stress on memory that the stressed retrieval practice **students performed better** than those who weren't stressed and had used the re-reading technique for their revision.

Ref: Smith et al, 2016, *Science*

THE ONE ABOUT RETRIEVAL PRACTICE AND STRESS

 ## RELATED RESEARCH

Stress has been found to impair memory because of an increase in cortisol released in the brain. This blocks the pathways near the hippocampus (the part of the brain largely responsible for memory), making it harder to recall things. Retrieval practice offers a way around this, as the act of having to generate an answer creates numerous and clear routes to accessing the information in our brain, essentially circumventing the stress blockade.

It is interesting to note that stress levels seem to be contagious, with two separate studies finding that parental stress level is often transferred to their child, as are teacher stress levels to their students. There is some evidence however to suggest that stress is not always a bad thing. Too little stress and people can feel lethargic and full of apathy. However, too much stress can lead to a reduction in memory because of excessive anxiety and narrowing of focus. It therefore appears that there is a Goldilocks level when it comes to stress, with just the right amount aiding performance.

CLASSROOM IMPLICATIONS

This study suggests that by teaching students the importance of retrieval, be it quizzes, essay answers, verbally answering a question or multiple choice tests (#91), we can not only help them learn the content at a faster rate, we can also help ensure that they can access this knowledge when they are under stress in the final exams.

The message to students couldn't be clearer or simpler: don't study in order to do well at the test. Do lots of tests in order to study well. By doing so, they will learn more and perform better under pressure. This means they will be able to deliver their best when it matters the most.

THE ONE ABOUT FALSE CONFIDENCE

@inner_drive | www.innerdrive.co.uk

THE STUDY

Researchers tested whether watching someone else perform a task gives an inaccurate and over-inflated sense of confidence that you can do it as well. They ran a series of studies that had participants watch other people successfully perform a range of tasks. These included doing the table cloth trick, moonwalking, playing darts and online video gaming. They then measured how confident the participants were at doing it themselves and then had them perform the task to assess the accuracy of their confidence.

THE MAIN FINDINGS

1 The more that people **watch someone else do a skill**, they more likely they are to believe **they can do it** as well.

2 **More doesn't always equal better.** Watching someone else many times did not improve actual ability relative to watching it once.

3 Interestingly, when people had to read about a task, or think about doing it, it **didn't increase their confidence**.

This increase in self-belief only occurred when watching someone else do it.

4 **This false confidence** from watching someone else many times comes from knowing "**what steps to take** but not how those **steps feel** when taking them".

Ref: Kardas and O'Brien, 2018, *Psychological Science*

THE ONE ABOUT FALSE CONFIDENCE

RELATED RESEARCH

Other evidence suggests that even watching a skilled performer from multiple angles and in slow motion is not enough to master a skill from sight alone, as "no matter how many times people watch a performance, they never gain one critical piece: the feeling of doing". Research does suggest that observing others is better than doing nothing, but to really develop talents and expertise requires many hours of deliberate practice.

A recent survey asked students which of the following five options would they first seek and then use most to help them learn new material. The options were a) watching others perform the task, b) reading about it or c) hearing the instructions. Overall, watching others perform was reported as the go-to strategy, the easiest to process and the most effective. The results from this study suggest that this may not be a wise choice. As the researchers of the study conclude, "while people may feel they are acquiring the skills that athletes, artists and technicians perform in front of their eyes, often these skills may be easier seen than done".

CLASSROOM IMPLICATIONS

Previous classroom research has indicated that it often is students who struggle the most who are more likely to have a false sense of confidence. This is referred to as the "Dunning-Kruger effect" (#18). This may be compounded by watching someone else perform a task successfully many times, as it results in a "misunderstanding of the kind and amount of practice needed during subsequent training and therefore be no better prepared".

This suggests that false confidence is the result of knowing the step-by-step guide of what to do but not having first-hand experience of actually doing it. The former breeds confidence, whereas the latter develops competence. Therefore, it is advisable that showing students what to do may be a good start, but for learning to be truly effective, they really need to practice it for themselves.

THE ONE ABOUT SOUND IN POWERPOINTS

@inner_drive | www.innerdrive.co.uk

THE STUDY

Researchers ran a series of studies to see if adding sounds to PowerPoint presentations improved learning. They taught students about various new concepts, such as the formation of lightning or the operation of hydraulic breaking systems. Some of the students received lessons that had background music, some had sounds (i.e. the sound of lightning would play), some had both and some had neither.

THE MAIN FINDINGS

1 Students who received **no background music or sounds** were able to recall

76% more than those who had a lesson that had both.

2 Groups who had lessons that had background music **learnt less than those who did not**. The latter was able to recall

11% more and did **29% better** on subsequent tests.

3 The results for students who had sounds as part of their lessons **were mixed**. Sometimes they did better but others they did worse. The authors note that **how these sounds are used is key**. "The more relevant and integrated sounds are, the more they will help students' understanding of the materials".

4 Students who liked listening to music and background noise **did not do any better** if their lessons had these. This suggests that their preference **does not accurately predict** what will help them learn more.

Ref: Moreno and Mayer, 2000, Journal of Educational Psychology.

THE ONE ABOUT SOUND IN POWERPOINTS

RELATED RESEARCH

There is a growing body of evidence that suggests that adding elements into a lesson that are intended to be entertaining, known as 'seductive details', actually hinders students' learning and subsequent performance. This is likely to be because students tend to remember the fun bits and not the important parts, as well as overloading their working memory capacity.

If teachers and students want to add material to either their lessons or revision, they would do well to pay heed to "dual-coding theory". This theory states that combining words and pictures represents both verbal and visual representation of the material, which therefore helps ingrain it into one's long term memory. This is different from this study, which found that adding music doesn't complement the material being learnt; it actually competed against it. Likewise, many students state that they prefer to revise whilst listening to music, as it makes the task less arduous. However, evidence suggest that this is a poor revision strategy which benefits very few whilst hindering many.

CLASSROOM IMPLICATIONS

This study is a potential huge time saver for anyone designing or delivering a lesson that uses a PowerPoint presentation. Even if the software offers a range of appealing and enticing animations, their use should be treated with caution. Essentially, the question everyone should ask themselves when creating new material is: "If it does not enhance learning, is it worth it?" Unless the answer is a definitive yes, then it is probably best to save yourself the time, effort and energy you will spend on implementing it.

The authors of the study end on a firm and defiant note by saying that "when presenting a multimedia explanation, only include complementary stimuli that are relevant to the content of the lesson" and that teachers "should carefully limit the amount of auditory material in multimedia lessons rather than add auditory materials for reasons of appeal and entertainment". Not only does it appear that less is more, but on many occasions, silence is in fact golden.

THE ONE ABOUT IDENTIFYING EXPERT TEACHERS

@inner_drive | www.innerdrive.co.uk

THE STUDY

It has often been said that teaching is the one profession that creates all other professions. Therefore it is important that we learn how to do it right. The ways that teachers learn from each other is an important part of this. Over a period of 5 years, teachers from 14 different primary schools were surveyed and interviewed to explore both how they discern each other's expertise and whether they are inclined to seek advice and help from the most able.

THE MAIN FINDINGS

1 The majority of teachers (over 90%) **did not refer to student test scores** when asked how to identify which of their colleagues were the best teachers.

2 Instead of focusing on test scores, teachers **judged their colleagues'** level of expertise on:

- ▶ The type of instruction they used when teaching
- ▶ The sort of questions they asked students during their lesson
- ▶ The organisation and flow of their lesson
- ▶ Their ability to generate student engagement
- ▶ Their subject knowledge

3 A teacher's performance based on student test scores **does not predict** whether they are asked for advice on teaching by their colleagues.

4 On the other hand, these "expert" teachers, as measured by student test scores, were the ones who were actually **more likely to seek advice from their peers** the following year. It seems that the better the teacher performed, the **more likely they were to go out and obtain feedback** on how to be even better.

Ref: Spillane et al. 2018.

THE ONE ABOUT IDENTIFYING EXPERT TEACHERS

 ## RELATED RESEARCH

The finding that the most able are not particularly sought after for their advice and are instead more likely to seek it from others is perhaps unsurprising. Other research on the Dunning-Kruger effect (#18) has found that the least able tend to have an inflated view of their abilities, which would presumably lead to them seeking out less feedback. After all, why would one seek out advice if you think there is little room for development?

Other research has explored the complexity of feedback, with one study viewing it as a 'double-edged sword' (#25). This is because it has been found that over a third of feedback interventions actually do more harm than good. This suggests that not only is the amount of feedback a factor, but also the quality. One study found that teachers are more likely to give feedback if students had been successful (compared to if they had failed) and on particular difficult tasks (#97).

One large-scale review (#52) offered good guidance on how best to deliver feedback, highlighting how at different times and at different stages of learning, feedback on the task, the strategy used, or the self-regulation of the student may be more important.

CLASSROOM IMPLICATIONS

Why did most of the teachers not use student test scores as a key factor when weighing up teaching expertise? The researchers suggested that "teachers do not trust student test scores as valid measures of teacher performance in general" or, if they do, that "student test scores may not easily be remembered or accessed as teachers make decisions about whom to seek for advice, especially if such decisions are made quickly during the work day". Essentially, weighing up teaching expertise was seen as something that you can sense, as opposed to being measurable by objective numerical data.

As for the findings that expert teachers are more likely to seek out advice and feedback, the researchers speculate that their advice-seeking tendencies may be explained as "they represent a group of teachers who are constantly striving to improve by seeking out advice and information from others". Creating an environment and culture where all staff appreciate, value and actively seek out feedback may be key to improving teaching standards, and therefore student educational attainment over large periods of time.

THE ONE ABOUT READING AND BACKGROUND NOISE

@inner_drive | www.innerdrive.co.uk

THE STUDY

One of the most popular revision strategies for students is to read and re-read their notes. A wealth of research over many years has highlighted that this is likely to be a fairly ineffective technique, nonetheless, it is still widely used. So, if students are going to read their notes, how can they do so in the most effective way? To find out, researchers conducted one of the largest literature reviews covering 65 different studies on the topic.

THE MAIN FINDINGS

1 Background speech, noise and music all had a **negative effect** on reading comprehension. This was true **for both children and adults**.

2 The researchers found that "there was a **95% probability** that lyrical music was **more distracting** than nonlyrical music".

3 Both background speech and music were **the biggest distraction** and are likely to be **just as distracting as each other**.

The researchers comment that **this is surprising** because "most people perceive lyrical music to be subjectively less distracting than intelligible speech".

Ref: Vasilev et al, 2018, Association for Psychological Science.

THE ONE ABOUT READING AND BACKGROUND NOISE

 ## RELATED RESEARCH

This study provides valuable insights as, despite being one of the most popular ways for students to revise for their exams, simply re-reading their notes is one of the least effective strategies (#1). Other research has highlighted how, if students are going to use reading as their primary source of learning, then they should read their notes out loud (#34). The finding that we should try to minimise background noise to aid reading comprehension, as it essentially competes for our attention, is supported by other research which found that listening to music that has lyrics whilst studying also has a detrimental effect on exam results (#17).

That said, reading is not done for the sole purpose of improving academic performance. Reading for pleasure has been associated with vocabulary development, greater exposure to a wider range of words, improving mental health, aiding a better night's sleep and reducing the decline of mental capacities in later life. Key to this is that our attitude towards reading for pleasure is heavily influenced in our formative years, which means both schools and parents play a very important role in shaping this (#54).

CLASSROOM IMPLICATIONS

Studies like these are highly valuable as a lot of both classroom and independent study time is spent reading. The researchers could not be clearer when they conclude their study by saying that their results "showed that background noise, speech and music are almost always distracting, even if the distraction effects are small in size". Given that several studies have found that more than 50% of students reported studying or doing homework with music in the background, these results could help alter their learning habits for the better.

Central to achieving this change would be following a three-step programme. Firstly, students should be encouraged to self-reflect on their current study habits to see if they are making avoidable errors. Secondly, we should help educate children on the potential costs of reading and revising in environments that have excessive background noises. Finally, interventions work best if there is ongoing support with them. This means that a one-off session on how to read effectively may yield some short-term gains, but with additional follow-up assistance, it can lead to long-term improvements as well.

THE ONE ABOUT TRANSITIONING TO SECONDARY SCHOOL

@inner_drive | www.innerdrive.co.uk

THE STUDY

The transition from primary to secondary school can be a difficult time for students. Young students have to deal with a new environment, an increase in the number of teacher relationships they need to form and an increased workload. Evidence suggests that the stress may lead to an initial reduction in grades and a more negative attitude to school.

Researchers recently explored how best to help students manage this transition. To help reduce any assessment bias, they ran a double-blind experiment, which is where the teachers implementing the intervention and the students receiving it are unaware if they are in the control or intervention group. In this study, the intervention group were given advice on how most struggle to fit in at first, how to engage in academic and social environments and they had confirmation that support was available. The students also had to reflect on how they would deal with hypothetical situations.

THE MAIN FINDINGS

1 Students in the intervention group reported:

 ‣ **Higher levels of school trust**
 ‣ **Social belonging**
 ‣ **Lower levels of anxiety**

2 The intervention group went on to receive **higher grades overall**, as well as **less numbers of low grades** (D's and F's).

3 Students in the intervention group had on average

12% fewer absences

and **34% fewer behavioural referrals** than those in the control group.

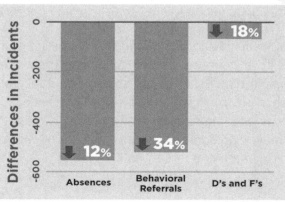

Ref: Borman et al. 2019. Proceedings of the National Academy of Sciences of the United States of America.

THE ONE ABOUT TRANSITIONING TO SECONDARY SCHOOL

RELATED RESEARCH

The transition from primary school to secondary school can feel especially daunting, as students at this age are already going through many physical and psychological changes. Other research suggests that this stress is magnified when joining a new school because of the increased work requirement; new, multiple teacher-student relationships and having to navigate larger buildings.

Several studies have found that the stress of starting secondary school often leads to an initial reduction in grades, decline in self-esteem and negative attitude towards teachers. One study suggested a potential route to navigating these challenges. Researchers from Columbia University and Stanford University tracked teenagers over two years and found evidence to suggest that a student's mindset affected how well they managed these transitions. They found that those with a growth mindset (#5, #68) were more likely to get higher grades, take on learning goals, value effort and adopt positive coping strategies and were less likely to feel helpless than students with a fixed mindset.

Transitions from one stage of education to another have also been studied in older students moving from secondary school to university. One recent study found that key to managing this change was keeping a sense of perspective, maintaining good physical health, and creating/maintaining support networks.

CLASSROOM IMPLICATIONS

Supporting students when they transition to secondary school should start when they are still in primary school. Previous research has found that taster days, giving out clear information to set expectations and using some of next year's material in advance are all helpful strategies. Likewise, evidence from this study suggests that pre-empting and removing some of the taboo of their worries (which typically include how most students are concerned that they won't fit in or how to behave) will help facilitate this transition.

Using hypothetical situations that students may have to deal with offers a good chance for teachers to get an insight into how their students are currently feeling. It also helps the students talk through and explore possible solutions which will help to normalise the new situation they find themselves in.

THE ONE ABOUT DRAWING FOR LEARNING

@inner_drive | www.innerdrive.co.uk

THE STUDY

The Production Effect states that if students create something new with the material they are learning from, it helps them to cement that content in their long-term memory. This has previously been studied by having students produce a lesson for other students or reading out loud (which 'produces' sounds from the words, instead of reading in silence).

But what about drawing pictures of what they were learning? Would this also count as an example of the Production Effect? Researchers from universities in Germany and America collaborated to find out. They compared students who simply read a key text with those who read and also drew pictures of it. They also tested to see whether drawing the picture themselves or having it given to them made a difference.

THE MAIN FINDINGS

1 Students who also drew pictures **performed significantly better** in the final tests. This was true for both their comprehension tests and when they had to replicate their drawings.

2 Students who also drew pictures **needed more learning time** (as it took them longer to produce their diagrams). However, additional analysis showed that **it was the act of drawing** and not just the additional learning time that **made them perform better.**

3 Students who also drew pictures **reported putting more effort into their learning.** This is likely to account for their improved performance.

4 Students who had to do their own drawing **performed better in subsequent tests** than those who had been given the diagram already finished.

Ref: Schmeck et al, 2014, Contemporary Educational Psychology.

THE ONE ABOUT DRAWING FOR LEARNING

 ## RELATED RESEARCH

The impact that drawing has on learning has been studied and replicated numerous times over the past 30 years. The researchers of this paper summarise these findings, explaining that "by drawing, learners are no longer passive consumers of information and knowledge; they are actively involved in the cognitive processes of selecting, organizing and integrating the information to be learned. Thus, learner-generated drawing is a cognitive learning strategy that is aimed to foster learning from the text, and if used adequately drawing can increase learning outcomes".

This is expanded upon later, when they summarised one of the seminal studies in this area by stating that there are three processes that aid this learning. "First, learners select the relevant key information from the text. Second, the selected key information is organized to build up an internal verbal representation of the text information. Third, learners construct an internal nonverbal (visual) representation of the text information and connect it with the verbal representation and with relevant prior knowledge". Essentially, and in layman's terms, it helps students select, organise and recall information, which helps cement it in their long-term knowledge.

CLASSROOM IMPLICATIONS

The researchers highlight how the students were given some prompts and structure on how to create their drawings in this experiment. This suggests that doing so may provide enough of a framework for students to work from but also enough autonomy for them to have to work hard at generating the diagrams themselves. This would be something for teachers to bear in mind if they are considering using this production effect for their students within their lessons.

Outside of lessons, this area of research could be useful for students when they are studying for a test. Mind-maps are often a very popular revision technique for students, but typically just contain words. This study suggests that incorporating pictures, drawings and diagrams may be an additional way to help them accelerate their learning.

THE ONE ABOUT EFFECTIVE TEACHER-STUDENT INTERACTIONS

@inner_drive | www.innerdrive.co.uk

THE STUDY

A good learning environment is easy to identify once you see it, but it is harder to describe it. This rather fascinating study explored the interactions between a teacher and their students, and then measured to see what impact this had on student test performance.

Researchers from the University of Virginia, Rugters University, University of Maryland and University of British Columbia tracked almost 2,000 students from over 100 classrooms and from 11 different schools to assess what teacher interactions contributed most to making an effective learning environment.

THE MAIN FINDINGS

1 After factoring in the **previous year's test performance,** qualities of teacher interactions with students **predicted student performance** on the end of year exams.

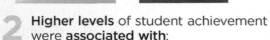

2 **Higher levels** of student achievement were **associated with**:

✓ **A positive emotional climate in the classroom:** including positive relationships and good communication.

✓ **Sensitivity to adolescent needs and perspectives:** high levels of empathy, flexibility and responsiveness.

✓ **The use of diverse and engaging instructional learning formats:** clear learning targets and range of activities.

✓ **A focus on analysis and problem solving:** developing student metacognition.

3 Effects of higher quality teacher–student interactions **were greatest in classrooms with fewer students.**

Ref: Allen et al. 2013, *School Psychology Review.*

THE ONE ABOUT EFFECTIVE TEACHER-STUDENT INTERACTIONS

 ## RELATED RESEARCH

The recent Program for International Student Assessment (PISA) review on schools worldwide supported some of the findings from this study, as it confirmed that having a "good disciplinary classroom climate" was a significant factor in helping disadvantaged students develop their academic resilience and overall educational attainment. Interestingly, though, this same review did not record similar findings for the impact of having smaller classroom sizes (#62).

Other research has also highlighted the importance of the teacher-student relationship. It has been shown to impact the levels of student engagement and influence how students perceive themselves and others in their class. It is interesting to note that teacher-student relationships are also a decent marker for teacher well-being. One study found that the higher the percentage of teacher-student relationships that a teacher judged to be negative, the higher their levels of stress and negative emotions were.

The finding that being attuned and sensitive to adolescent needs and their perspectives is a key factor in teacher-student interactions is interesting as many studies have found that the teenage brain is very different to that of an adult (#8). Some notable differences between them include attitudes to risk taking, social status, self-control and self-regulation.

CLASSROOM IMPLICATIONS

The authors of this study highlight how "engaging adolescent students emotionally may be critical to maximizing their academic motivation in the classroom". This suggests that it is not just the 'what' we teach them that matters, but also the how and the why. Previous research gives an indication on how to do this, with studies finding that creating a sense of purpose (#14), asking pre-questions (#69) and developing their metacognitive skills (#84) can all help do this.

THE ONE ABOUT HOW METACOGNITION HELPS

@inner_drive | www.innerdrive.co.uk

THE STUDY

Metacognition, which the researchers of this paper state covers areas such as "self-regulated learning", "thinking skills" and "learning to learn", has become an increasingly popular topic within education. A recent review of the existing psychological research looked at what impact metacognition has on students and how best to develop it.

THE MAIN FINDINGS

1 **Metacognitive strategies have been associated with**:

✔ **Better academic performance** - some research highlighting this is especially true for Maths, though the researchers state that "wherever metacognitive skills are taught in lessons, there appears to be **improvement in pupil outcomes**, irrespective of which subjects are being taught".

✔ **Positive motivation cycle** – "greater motivation leads to improved metacognition, which leads to greater motivation".

2 **Who benefits?**

✔ **Metacognitive interventions** have been found to be **successful with students from primary age** through to university students.

✔ It can be of **great benefit to disadvantaged and struggling students**, and for those who exhibit challenging behaviour.

THINK SMARTER THINK BETTER

3 **How best to deliver metacognitive strategies:**

✔ **Embed it across the whole curriculum** rather than in discrete lessons.

✔ The purpose of the learning and of the **metacognitive strategies should be explicitly taught**.

✔ **Don't rush it:** it works best over a longer period of time.

4 **The Limitations**

✔ Metacognition is very **difficult to measure**.

✔ We know more **about what metacognition is correlated** with, rather than "the causalities". This means nuance, **context and further research is needed**.

Ref: Perry et al, 2019, Educational Review.

THE ONE ABOUT HOW METACOGNITION HELPS

RELATED RESEARCH

Other research has highlighted two different types of metacognition. One is "metacognitive knowledge", which refers to a student's awareness of what they do or don't know (i.e. their strengths, weaknesses and gaps in their knowledge). The other is "metacognitive regulation", which refers to the different strategies that students may use to manage their thoughts and emotions. Developing both could be vitally important and illustrates how metacognition is more than just its common definition of "thinking about your thinking".

Evidence suggests that, as well as being potentially one of the most effective strategies to help students improve their academic achievements, metacognition may also be one of the most cost-effective ones as well. This has been documented across a range of subjects, including maths, science, English and music. Beyond academic performance, other research papers have found that it can help improve self-awareness which may affect both novice/struggling students (#18) as well as those with high abilities/expertise (#43).

CLASSROOM IMPLICATIONS

The researchers of this study acknowledge that metacognition can be difficult to define and categorise. They state, that "because metacognition has such a fuzzy quality, there is no agreed typology of metacognitive strategies used in the classroom. However, most educators would include strategies that help pupils to monitor, plan, evaluate and regulate their performance, whilst completing a particular task, as well as strategies that consciously help pupils solve novel problems".

Indeed, one previous study (#61) found that by having students ask themselves three meta-cognitive questions: "Which resources do I need to help me study?", "Why are those resources helpful?" and "How will I use these resources?", their self-reflection, emotional control and exam performance improved.

Other ways to do this could be to encourage students to reflect on what did and didn't work well and to reflect on what they would do differently next time. The challenge with this is that in the short term it takes more time; however, in the long run, it leads to a much bigger and more positive pay-out.

THE ONE ABOUT PARENTAL INVOLVEMENT

@inner_drive | www.innerdrive.co.uk

THE STUDY

An area of research that has long interested many people is how parental involvement in a child's education can impact their academic achievements. Parental involvement can be defined and measured in several ways but is generally seen as a combination of how engaged parents are at home and with the school, and how positive their attitudes are towards their child's education, school and teachers.

One study that shed some light on this area tracked various factors on 158 primary-aged students. These included the level of parental involvement, student IQ, academic performance, perceived academic competence and teacher–student relationships. These were measured using both standardised tests and by teachers filling in questionnaires.

THE MAIN FINDINGS

1 Parental involvement was **positively associated with student's academic performance** in the classroom, over and beyond the variance accounted for by the child's IQ.

2 After **controlling for a child's IQ**, parental involvement was **positively associated** with:

✔ **Students having good relationships with their teachers.**

✔ **How students perceive their own cognitive ability.**

3 Once the student–teacher relationship was accounted for, parental involvement **did not predict** the child's academic performance. This highlights the **importance of the teacher–student relationship**.

The researchers do point out that **there are several limitations to their study**, notably that several of the measures that were being monitored were taken based on the teacher's perception and opinion. This may have led to **some inaccuracies**, "specifically, it may be that some teachers were unduly influenced by outside factors, such as the parent being involved in the school's PTA and were unable to determine the parent's actual attitude toward the child's education".

Ref: Topor et al. 2010, *Journal of Prevention & Intervention in the Community.*

THE ONE ABOUT PARENTAL INVOLVEMENT

 ## RELATED RESEARCH

There is a wealth of research that highlights the positive link between parental involvement and a child's academic performance. Indeed, there is evidence to suggest that parental beliefs about their child's academic ability carries more weight in their child's mind than their actual exam results (#46).

One such study (#11) found that having high academic expectations and regular communication were two of the most important parental behaviours and made the most impact on academic achievement. Parents should tread carefully, though, as it is not always a case of more being better. For example, one study (#64) found that parental over-involvement with homework was an unhelpful strategy, and those students who completed their homework by themselves performed more than 10% better in their final exam.

The finding from this study that parental involvement was positively associated with teacher-student relationships is an interesting and important one, given that there is lot of research that highlights the numerous positive benefits for students and teachers to have a healthy dynamic (#83). Therefore, anything that encourages this should be welcomed by all.

CLASSROOM IMPLICATIONS

The researchers of this study suggest that schools should "investigate ways to increase a parent's positive attitude about their child's education and demonstrate to parents that their attitude is related to their child's academic performance".

However, there doesn't appear to be one set way of doing this, as "longitudinal studies are needed to understand how these variables interact over time". Therefore, the findings from this study, whilst in sync with previous research, should be viewed with this perspective in mind. For now, parent evenings, newsletters, and school programmes are likely to offer the best route.

THE ONE ABOUT BAD DECISION MAKING

@inner_drive | www.innerdrive.co.uk

THE STUDY

Why do students make decisions in the present that won't make them happy in the future? This dilemma is particularly pertinent for students who have to revise for exams that will have a significant impact on their lives. They know how important their exams will be, yet they don't always make good decisions in the present when it comes to preparation and revision. If we knew why this happened, then perhaps we would be better placed to help inform and guide students during these key periods of their education.

Fortunately, researchers specialising in thinking biases have investigated this for many years. Combining decades of research, psychologists from the University of Chicago have summarised why we make decisions and choose experiences that don't make us happy in the long run.

THE MAIN FINDINGS

People fail to make optimal decisions because a) they fail to predict future experiences accurately and b) they fail to follow through with their intentions.

1 Causes of Failure to Predict Future Experiences

Impact Bias
People **often over-estimate** the intensity and duration of positive events. This means **we think the highs will be higher** and last for longer.

Projection Bias
We **project our current feelings on to future events**, even when they are not relevant. As an example, the researchers state that "when people predict immediately after dinner how much they will enjoy a delicious breakfast the next morning, they understate the pleasure. They appear to reason as if because they are full now, they will also be full the next morning".

Memory Bias
When predicting future events, **we draw on how we felt about similar things** in the past. But past memories are fallible and are often susceptible to manipulation and riddled with inaccuracies.

2 Failure to Follow Through on Intentions

Impulsivity
The **ability to delay gratification is hard**. Many would rather have less of a good thing now than more of the same thing in the long-term.

Rule-Based Decisions
Sticking rigidly to rules or what one thinks one 'ought to do' or 'should do' **can lead to people being too rigid** and **not doing what is right for them** in that particular context.

Ref: Hsee and Hastie (2006). Trends in Cognitive Science.

THE ONE ABOUT BAD DECISION MAKING

 ## RELATED RESEARCH

This study neatly categorises two of the reasons that cause people to make poor decisions: we are bad at predicting the future and are bad at following through with our intentions. In terms of being bad at predicting future behaviour, these findings chime with previous research that found that we are not very good at guessing how long a task will take (#2). This is partially because we have a poor perception of time and suffer from a memory bias that over-values how we temporarily feel at the end of an experience or event (#98).

With regards to not following through on our intentions, evidence suggests that it often isn't sufficient simply to be motivated at the start of a task (#6). To convert intentions into behaviour change, the ability to delay gratification is important (#13, #31). By suffering a little in the short term, we can prosper more in the long term. As we are highly drawn to instant rewards, this can be difficult, and there is evidence to suggest that some find it harder than others to delay gratification because of differences in their brains. Fortunately, other research has suggested ways to improve this; for example, if students trust the person giving them the instructions and if their environment is consistently reliable, it can help improve the ability to delay gratification.

CLASSROOM IMPLICATIONS

As students become older and progress through the education system, their ability to study independently becomes more important. These times of self-directed study, whether at home or during study-periods can have a big impact on their exams (and indeed their future lives). Therefore, any evidence that can help them to make better long-term choices is very much welcomed.

By helping students to reflect on previous events and to project how they might feel in the future based on different outcomes, offers a good route to doing this. Likewise, removing short-term distractions, getting plenty of sleep (#29, #92) and effective goal setting can help develop their impulse control.

THE ONE ABOUT AGE AND ACADEMIC SELF-CONCEPT

@inner_drive | www.innerdrive.co.uk

THE STUDY

How much impact does being born early or late in the school year have on a child's performance? Previous research on primary-aged students suggests this impact may be quite significant. This is not surprising given that the oldest child in a year group can be as much as a 20% older than the youngest at the beginning of primary school.

In terms of academic ability, the impact of this age gap reduces as students get older. But what effect does it have on students' self-belief in their academic abilities? Researchers recently tested this by monitoring the age, self-beliefs and university applications of over 10,000 15-year-old Australian students.

THE MAIN FINDINGS

1 Compared to their peers, **students who are older** within the school year, **rate themselves higher** in:

✔ **Maths ability**

✔ **English ability**

✔ **Overall academic ability**

2 Controlling for actual academic achievement, **being one of the younger students in the year was a negative predictor** of going to university.

3 However, **if self-belief levels, which are malleable, are high,** then being young in the school year does not have any significant impact.

Ref: Parker et al. 2019. *Journal of Educational Psychology.*

THE ONE ABOUT AGE AND ACADEMIC SELF-CONCEPT

 ## RELATED RESEARCH

The Relative Age Effect is a term used to describe how those born early in the academic year tend to perform to a higher level than those born later. One study of children ages 5-7 found a relationship between the month a child was born in and their performance in a phonics test, with those being born at the start of the school year performing significantly better.

Indeed, evidence from the Education Datalab highlights how the Relative Age Effect is more pronounced in primary students compared with secondary ones. This is partly because, the younger you are, the difference between being born at the start of the school year compared with the end is a higher percentage of your total age.

Research from outside of education suggests that this effect is more widespread than many may have thought. Recent work on this effect in sport, which combined the findings of 38 different studies spanning 23 years, 14 sports and 16 countries, found that for every two participants born in the last quarter of an annual age group, there were more than three participants who were born in the first quarter. More specifically, the researchers discovered that the youngest within the year group were less likely to participate in both recreational and competitive sport from under the age of 14, to play at a regional or national standard aged 15-18, or to become an elite athlete.

CLASSROOM IMPLICATIONS

The Relative Age Effect may have a slight self-fulfilling prophecy to it. Being born late in the year means that these students are physically, emotionally and cognitively behind their elder peers to start with. But, if this leads to these students being viewed either as not as smart or having behavioural difficulties, then this label can stick to them. This in turn could lead to teachers, parents and indeed themselves, viewing themselves through this lens whilst also believing that it is a permanent feature of their personality. Therefore, it is advisable when giving feedback to focus on the task, the child's processes and the child's self-regulation, instead of on them as a person (#52).

THE ONE ABOUT SELF-REGULATED LEARNING

@inner_drive | www.innerdrive.co.uk

THE STUDY

Years and years of research in cognitive psychology has found that some revision strategies, such as retrieval practice and spacing, are far more effective than others like cramming and simply re-reading notes.

This may be what past research tells us, but recently researchers wanted to find out how likely students are to select the best strategies for themselves when revising. Also, what impact does their mindset have on these choices, along with their motivation to revise well and ability to do so efficiently?

THE MAIN FINDINGS

1 The **most popular revision strategy** was to re-read information, with **75%** **of students** stating they did this lots.

2 66% of participants indicated that they **used a form of retrieval practice**; with **flashcards (40%)** and **self-testing (46%)** being the two most prominent.

3 Students were just as likely to **space out their revision (39%)** as they were to **cram their revision (36%)**.

4 61% of students **reported that they study whatever topic or subject is due soonest**, with only **20% prioritising and studying** in the areas they are the weakest at. This suggests that students **tend to be motivated by deadlines** rather than by managing their revision.

5 Students with a growth mindset were **more likely to value the effective revision strategies**, such as retrieval practice, compared to less effective strategies, such as simply re-reading their notes.

6 Students with a growth mindset were also **more likely to be intrinsically motivated to do their revision**, and those with a fixed mindset were more likely to need extrinsic motivation.

Ref: Yan et al. 2014. Journal of Applied Research in Memory and Cognition.

THE ONE ABOUT SELF-REGULATED LEARNING

 ## RELATED RESEARCH

This study builds on previous research which has helped to rank which study strategies are the most effective (#1). The previous research had found that the likes of retrieval practice (#23, #76), spacing (#4) and interleaving (#15, #96) are better strategies than simply re-reading notes. However, this study now allows us to compare the most effective strategies with the most popular ones. Doing so is of great interest and value, as it suggests that, unfortunately for many students, the most commonly used strategy is actually the least effective.

This study also builds on previous research done on growth mindset (#5). To date, a lot of this research has focused on how students with a different mindset feel, with evidence suggesting that those with a growth mindset have higher self-esteem, stronger effort levels and more emotional stability with regards to their academic performance (#68). This study, as far as we are aware, is the first to link mindset with revision techniques.

CLASSROOM IMPLICATIONS

The researchers of this study summarise part of their findings by stating that "individuals who believe that intelligence can be increased through effort were more likely to value the pedagogical benefits of self-testing, to restudy and to be intrinsically motivated to learn". They do urge some caution when interpreting their findings, as "the research we report is correlational", but note that "it is likely that effective self-regulated learning requires both understanding of what learning strategies are effective and an appreciation that effort and difficulty are central to the process of learning, rather than a sign of failure to learn".

This suggests that schools can adopt a two-pronged approach to helping their students to study better. Firstly, they can educate their students on the different types of study strategies, highlighting both the benefits of them, and how to effectively do them. Secondly, by helping students attribute their success to internal causes such as effort and studying, students can develop their mindset towards intrinsic motivation, which is a more robust and reliable form of motivation in the long term.

THE ONE ABOUT COGNITIVE LOAD

@inner_drive | www.innerdrive.co.uk

THE STUDY

Cognitive Load Theory highlights how working memory is limited, and if it is overloaded, then the transfer of information from working memory to long-term memory is hindered. This has an effect on the amount that students learn.

Having to receive information from two or more sources can place a burden on working memory, as focus is being spread too thinly. This is known as the Split-Attention Effect. In order to investigate this, researchers tested to see if students who were presented with 'integrated' diagrams (i.e. information imbedded within the diagram) performed better than those who were given 'conventional' diagrams with the additional information below it.

THE MAIN FINDINGS

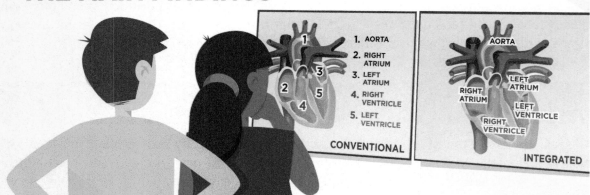

1. AORTA
2. RIGHT ATRIUM
3. LEFT ATRIUM
4. RIGHT VENTRICLE
5. LEFT VENTRICLE

CONVENTIONAL

INTEGRATED

1 Students who were given information in an **integrated diagram took less time to process** the information than those who had to alternate between instructions and conventional diagrams.

2 Students who were given **integrated diagrams** also **performed better** on the exam, getting on average **22%** higher marks.

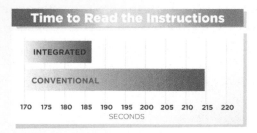

Time to Read the Instructions

INTEGRATED

CONVENTIONAL

170 175 180 185 190 195 200 205 210 215 220
SECONDS

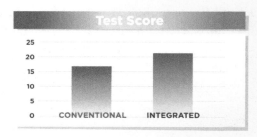

Test Score

25
20
15
10
5
0

CONVENTIONAL   INTEGRATED

Ref: Chandler and Sweller, 1992, British *Journal of Educational Psychology*.

THE ONE ABOUT COGNITIVE LOAD

RELATED RESEARCH

This study is one of the seminal research papers that contributes to our understanding of Cognitive Load Theory. It builds on one of the most iconic psychological studies on working memory, which found that found that when participants were presented with a series of numbers one at a time on a screen, they could only accurately recall a sequence of seven items, plus or minus two.

This current study has been referred to as the Split-Attention Effect, which forms a part of Cognitive Load Theory, as it highlights how asking students to split their attention between two sources simultaneously, causes cognitive overload (#41). Another part of Cognitive Load Theory is the Redundancy Effect, in which giving students irrelevant information whilst they are learning something clogs up their working memory. This means students remember the wrong information, rather than the information you want them to remember. Research suggests that, amongst other strategies, this effect can be avoided by limiting PowerPoint animations (#78), avoiding excessive classroom decorations (#93) and not revising whilst listening to music that has lyrics (#17).

CLASSROOM IMPLICATIONS

A student's working memory can be seriously affected if they are receiving information from two or more places. Switching between different sources can lead to students remembering less content because their energy and resources are spent trying to process several things at the same time. This is why using integrated diagrams over traditional ones can be so helpful.

If a teacher is presenting complex content (i.e. information that students have no previous experience with), then the more that students need to split their attention, the more likely it is that cognitive overload will occur. If the material is easy to understand or has been encountered by students many times before, teachers could then gradually increase the complexity of the material.

Cognitive Load Theory is not without some challenges. It is notoriously hard (maybe impossible) to realistically measure cognitive load, and in a class of 30 students in which each one has their own optimum load, striking the right balance is difficult. It is also worth noting that Cognitive Load Theory talks about optimising load, not necessarily reducing it. The best way to think about it is through the Goldilocks Effect - the amount has to be just right. Too much cognitive load means that information will get lost, while too little cognitive load means that students just won't learn enough.

THE ONE ABOUT THE EFFECTS OF SCREEN TIME

@inner_drive | www.innerdrive.co.uk

THE STUDY

Students are growing up with an ever increasing range of electronic devices at their disposal. This includes phones, TVs, computers and tablets. As such, it is an area of great concern for teachers and parents alike.

But what does the evidence say about the cost of screen time? It is not possible to say how much time spent in front of a screen is too much, however a recent review of the existing research did highlight some very interesting findings.

THE MAIN FINDINGS

1 There is a **strong link** between **more screen time** and:

✓ **The Likelihood of being obese**
✓ **Depressive symptoms**

2 There is **moderate evidence** linking **more screen time** and:

✓ **Less healthy diets**
✓ **Eating foods with a high energy density**
✓ **Poorer quality of life**

3 There is **weak evidence** linking **more screen** time and:

✓ **Behavioural problems**
✓ **Anxiety**
✓ **Hyper-activeness and inattention**
✓ **Lower fitness levels**
✓ **Worse sleep**

4 The researchers also found that **small amounts of daily screen time** are not harmful and may have some benefits.

Ref: Stiglic and Viner, 2019, BMJ.

THE ONE ABOUT THE EFFECTS OF SCREEN TIME

 ## RELATED RESEARCH

A different study, which examined 40,000 students between ages 2-17, found that greater hours of screen time were associated with lower well-being. Those students with a greater amount of screen time (7+ hours a day) often suffer from less curiosity, a lack of self-control and emotional instability. The same study found that even a moderate use of screens (4 hours a day) is associated with a lower psychological well-being.

Most of the research on the impact on screen time on adolescents has focused on televisions, with less being centred on computers and mobile phones. However, studies are starting to emerge on the latter two technologies. For example, evidence suggests that schools that ban mobile phones get a significant boost to their exam results (#49). This could be in part due to the negative impact that phones have on concentration levels (#30). Other research has also noted the negative impact phones have on sleep if they are used up to two hours before bedtime (#40).

With regards to the findings that show a weak association between screen time and behavioural problems, anxiety, reduced fitness levels and sleep, the researchers do emphasise that "it is important to note that the weak evidence reported here largely relates to a lack of literature rather than weak associations". This suggests that more research is needed before we can draw firm conclusions.

CLASSROOM IMPLICATIONS

Enthusiasm for technology in the classroom runs the risk of going beyond what we currently know about the impact that it might have. It can clearly have some benefits, such as access to information and remote learning. However, it does have some drawbacks. For example, one study (#72) found that students who take notes electronically typically do worse when they have to put this learning into practice (although this finding has not always been replicated).

Given the potential negative effects that this study associated with screen time, it is easy to see how students may be exposed to mixed messages if, on the one hand, they are taught that too much screen time is bad, and, on the other hand, they are encouraged to use the technology a lot in class. Hopefully, more research can help guide us on how to walk this fine line.

THE ONE ABOUT PERFECT MULTIPLE-CHOICE TESTS

THE STUDY

@inner_drive | www.innerdrive.co.uk

Low-stakes quizzes (a way to use retrieval practice) are one of the most effective ways to improve learning and memory. Multiple-choice tests are one such tool to do so. But what makes the perfect multiple-choice test? Do some questions, formats and answers work better than others?

A recent study from Washington University reviewed all of the existing research and came up with some simple, practical and very useful suggestions.

THE MAIN FINDINGS

1 KEEP THINGS SIMPLE
Complex questions/answers can lead to students guessing. This means they might get it right by luck. Keeping the format simple **makes it a more reliable assessment** of a student's knowledge.

2 BE TARGETED
Create questions that **focus on specific parts** of knowledge or thought processes that you want to assess.

3 AVOID USING "NONE OF THE ABOVE"
If this is the correct answer, then the question has exposed students to incorrect answers that **they may remember as being true**. For similar reasons avoid using "All of the Above" as an answer.

4 GIVE 3 POTENTIAL ANSWERS TO THE QUESTION
This provides enough difficulty whilst also being time efficient.

5 AIM FOR "MODERATELY DIFFICULT"
If the test is too easy or too hard, then little will be learnt. The researcher states that if there are **three potential answers** to each question, around a 75% success rate is a good sweet-spot.

6 PROVIDE FEEDBACK
The researcher stated that "the **effectiveness of feedback** depends upon students being motivated to process it and their motivation tends to decrease over time". Therefore, if feedback is delayed, it would be wise to take steps to ensure that students are "required or incentivised to process it".

Ref: Butler, 2018, *Journal of Applied Research in Memory and Cognition*

THE ONE ABOUT PERFECT MULTIPLE-CHOICE TESTS

 ## RELATED RESEARCH

This recent paper sheds light on a very interesting area of research. The author of the study notes that, while some of the previous research focused on assessments in general ("avoid trick questions, omit irrelevant information, use simple vocabulary"), much of it is applicable directly to multiple-choice tests ("make each possible answer to a question the same length and rotate the position of the correct answer across items").

For example, one area that shows promise, is having students assign a confidence rating to their answer, as this helps to measure partial knowledge. This could help develop students' metacognitive knowledge and help them to highlight what areas they need to study further. However, the exact format for doing this is yet to be conclusively studied.

CLASSROOM IMPLICATIONS

This paper has useful implications for anyone designing multiple-choice tests. Given the amount of times that students complete quizzes as part of their classroom work or during homework, and how the right type of multiple-choice tests can help their learning, this is something certainly worth considering.

The ideal number of possible answers provided to a question is a fascinating finding, as by limiting it to around three, it has the added advantage of potentially saving a teacher time when designing questionnaires. Given that teacher time is one of the most precious resources that a school has, any strategy that aids learning while reducing the teacher time spent preparing would be welcomed by all.

The key to maximising any retrieval practice strategies is to ensure that they are done in a stress-free or 'low-stakes' environment. This is because excessive stress can significantly hinder memory (#76), meaning any advantage gained from doing quizzes may be somewhat negated if the quiz causes too much stress or anxiety. One way to mitigate this stress is to highlight to students that this is being done to aid and accelerate their learning, as opposed to being a judgement or a measurement of learning.

THE ONE ABOUT PARENTS AND SLEEP

@inner_drive | www.innerdrive.co.uk

THE STUDY

The importance of regularly getting a good night's sleep shouldn't be underestimated. Decades of research has found it to be associated with better grades, attention, memory, mood, health and well-being. Yet despite this, many students aren't getting anywhere near the recommended amount. This can be challenging for educators, as it not only impacts the daily lives of their students, but it is something that they have little control over.

Therefore, good sleeping habits are something that every parent should be thinking about for their child. But how accurate are parents at predicting how much sleep their child actually gets? To test this, researchers from Australia compared how much sleep 300 teenagers said they had had, with how much their parents estimated they were getting.

THE MAIN FINDINGS

1 On a school night:

✔ Parents thought their child was going to bed **around 15-20 minutes earlier** each night than they actually were.

✔ Parents thought their child slept for almost **9 hours a night**, but students were getting much **nearer 8 hours**.

✔ Parents were pretty accurate at knowing **what time their child woke up in the morning.**

2 On the weekend:

✔ Parents thought their child was going to bed **between 20-30 minutes earlier** than they actually were.

✔ Parents thought their child slept for almost **10 hours a night**. In reality they were actually getting **significantly less** than that.

✔ **Parents thought** their child was waking up later than they actually were – with some estimates being **almost an hour out.**

3 Overall, students **went to bed later, slept longer and woke up later** on the weekend than on school days.

Ref: Short et al, 2013. *Nature and Science of Sleep.*

THE ONE ABOUT PARENTS AND SLEEP

 ## RELATED RESEARCH

Other research has highlighted common sleep mistakes that students make. These include being on their phones/tablets too much (#40), going to bed at different times, napping for too long in the day, drinking high-energy drinks late at night and over-thinking what they have to do tomorrow. Given the importance of sleep (#29), it is necessary to explore how we can encourage students to get more of it.

A recent study may have highlighted one way. They investigated whether older students, if incentivised to get more sleep during exam periods, would sleep more and, if so, if this would lead to higher grades. The researchers offered extra credit to students who slept for at least 8 hours a night regularly (it should be noted that, for younger teenagers, this is still lower than the recommended amount). The researchers found that 71% of students who opted in to the 8-hour deal got the required amount of sleep and got higher marks than those who did not (even when the extra credit marks were taken into account).

CLASSROOM IMPLICATIONS

The researchers note that "given many biopsychosocial factors which predispose adolescents to later sleep-onset time, plus the propensity for adolescents to access computers, mobile phones and music players after bedtime, parents may not be in a position to provide accurate estimates of sleep". This is important, as the evidence from this study shows "that adolescent sleep is likely to be much more restricted than their parents believe" but that they may be "unlikely to act if they are not aware that their teens are not obtaining sufficient sleep".

Therefore, it is vital to educate both parents and students on the benefits of sleep, how to avoid common sleep mistakes and how to proactively cultivate a better and more beneficial nighttime routine. For students this may take the form of newsletters and discussions in tutorial times, whereas for parents, newsletters and parents evenings offer a more viable route.

THE ONE ABOUT CLASSROOM DECORATIONS

@inner_drive | www.innerdrive.co.uk

THE STUDY

Classroom displays are a common feature in many schools. They often include classroom rules, tips and strategies and showcase students' best work. This can all have a positive effect on how students feel and on their motivation levels. But is there a cost to this that's worth considering?

To find out, researchers from Carnegie Mellon University ran a study comparing primary-aged students who were taught in a highly-decorated classroom to those who were taught in a non-decorated classroom. They then measured how long they were distracted for, what distracted them the most, and how much they learnt over a two-week period.

THE MAIN FINDINGS

1 Students who were taught in the highly visually decorated classroom **were more distracted** by their environment.

They were distracted **20.56%** of the time compared to those in the **non-decorated classroom** (3.21%).

DISTRACTED BY THEIR ENVIRONMENT

Bar chart — Y-axis: % TIME DISTRACTED (0–25); X-axis categories: HIGHLY DECORATED (~20.5), NOT DECORATED (~3).

2 Students **who were in the non-decorated** classroom were **more likely to distract themselves** and be distracted by their peers, but were **still less likely to be distracted overall**, as the level of decoration was such a major factor.

3 Students in the highly-decorated classroom **spent more time off-task** (38.5% of the time) compared to those in the **non-decorated classroom** (28.42%).

4 Students in the highly-decorated classroom **made fewer learning gains in their final exam** than those who were taught in the non-decorated classroom.

■ First Test ■ Final Exam

Bar chart — Y-axis: % CORRECT (0–100); X-axis categories: SPARSE-CLASSROOM CONDITION (First Test ~20, Final Exam ~88), DECORATED-CLASSROOM CONDITION (First Test ~22, Final Exam ~41).

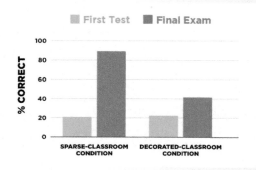

Ref: Fisher et al. 2014. *Psychological Science.*

THE ONE ABOUT CLASSROOM DECORATIONS

RELATED RESEARCH

This is a relatively new study, and as such, it is an under-researched area of educational psychology. Therefore, there is not a lot of related research. Indeed, even this pioneering study only used a small sample size of young students. Other research into student concentration intensity and direction has tended to focus more on the students themselves, as opposed to this study which looked at their environment. From these previous studies (#48), we know that for students, a large percentage of the lesson is spent being distracted or daydreaming.

One possible reason for the visual displays being too distracting for students is the limitations of their working memory, which researchers say is more pronounced in younger children. This means the visual displays compete for their attention, which creates a cognitive overload (#89). This then clogs up working memory, making it harder for relevant information to be transferred from working memory to long-term memory.

CLASSROOM IMPLICATIONS

The researchers of this study note that "the relationship between student age and typical classroom design is somewhat paradoxical. Younger learners are often placed in learning environments that are rich with potential sources of distractions (e.g. colourful educational materials and other visual displays). The problem is compounded because kindergarten and elementary school students receive the majority of instruction in a single classroom (i.e. they do not have a specialised classroom for each subject, as is common in middle and high school). Therefore, students are exposed to large amounts of visual materials that are not relevant for the ongoing instruction".

This is not to say that classroom decorations and stimuli can't be useful, just that they need to be targeted and well thought out. The researchers note that they are "not advocating sterilizing the learning environments of young children by removing all decorations, artwork or educational displays". Instead, it is all about finding the sweet spot between a helpful teaching aid and a potential distractor. This may include telling them which poster on the wall will be helpful for a particular task or only having the back wall decorated.

THE ONE ABOUT SUMMER LEARNING LOSS

@inner_drive | www.innerdrive.co.uk

THE STUDY

School summer holidays can be traced back to the Middle Ages; this was a time when there were many 'holy-days' and, with our agricultural history, many children were required to labour in the fields of their family farm during the summer months. But what impact do summer holidays have on a student's learning nowadays? And does it affect all students and all subjects equally? The seminal research, from over 20 years ago, which extensively reviewed the literature on this, makes for interesting reading.

THE MAIN FINDINGS

1 The impact of the summer holidays:

▶ On average, **students regressed** by the equivalent of **one month** over the summer holidays.

▶ Students' **maths ability suffered the most** from summer learning loss. **Reading skills** are also negatively affected, but not by quite so much.

2 Who is affected by the summer learning loss?

▶ Evidence suggests that **middle class students do not suffer** from summer learning loss **as much as students from lower classes.**

▶ Summer learning **loss is not impacted** by a student's race or gender.

3 Why does summer learning loss occur differentially?

▶ The **range of activities that students are exposed to** during the summer holidays (e.g. it is easier to practice reading than it is to practice maths).

▶ The **way different types of knowledge decay over time**; "fact and procedure-based knowledge is more easily forgotten than conceptual knowledge".

Ref: Cooper et al, 1996, *Review of Educational Research.*

THE ONE ABOUT SUMMER LEARNING LOSS

 ## RELATED RESEARCH

The Summer Learning Loss phenomenon makes sense given the wealth of evidence that has found the significant impact that student absenteeism has on educational achievement. Research from the Department of Education recently found that every day missed by students was associated with a reduced chance of attaining five or more A*-C's at GCSEs. It therefore is unsurprising that there is such a cost to having six consecutive weeks off school.

Other research has explored deeper into which students suffer the most during the summer. In support of this study's findings, researchers have found that students from lower socio-economic backgrounds feel the effects the most. Counterintuitively, there is some evidence to suggest that students with an exceptional ability are also likely to significantly suffer.

Since this landmark study, subsequent research has focused on interventions to help reduce the decline in learning over the summer holidays. Two positive areas include summer schools and joint reading programmes that crucially engage both students and their parents.

CLASSROOM IMPLICATIONS

How can schools best help mitigate against the effects of Summer Learning Loss? The researchers of this study note the different impact it has on different subjects and state that "the finding that subject area influenced the amount of summer loss may be due to the differential availability of opportunities to practice different academic material over the summer (with reading practice more available than math practice)". They therefore suggest setting students specific maths tasks, as well as providing support for parents so that they can assist their children.

It is concerning to note that this study found that "the income differences also may be related to differences in opportunities to practice and learn (with books and reading opportunities more available to middle class students to use)". Of course, individual differences exist, and one should guard against making sweeping generalisations, but any extra support schools can give to struggling or disadvantaged students should help reduce the negative impact that the summer holidays brings to their overall learning.

THE ONE ABOUT KNOWING THE END IS NEAR

@inner_drive | www.innerdrive.co.uk

THE STUDY

Students have to work hard in order to do well in their exams and meet coursework deadlines. Some struggle with this as they can't see an end in sight. So, does knowing how much longer is left in the task help students to perform better during it? Surprisingly, this hasn't been researched much before.

To rectify this, researchers from the Tel Aviv University recently ran a study where, over two experiments, they had students complete a new, complex and boring learning task. They divided students into two groups; one group was updated on how much of the task was left and the other group wasn't.

THE MAIN FINDINGS

The researchers found that if students knew how much of the task was left to do, compared to their peers who did not know, they:

1 Learnt at a **faster rate** and so achieved a **higher performance** quicker.

2 Felt **less fatigued** over the course of the task.

3 Took **shorter breaks** while completing the task – the researchers suggest that this was because "**knowing the end is near enhances motivation**". This was most pronounced towards the end of the tasks, where **those who were unaware** of how much time was left took breaks that were **up to twice as long** as those were aware.

Ref: Katzir et al, 2020. Cognition.

THE ONE ABOUT KNOWING THE END IS NEAR

 RELATED RESEARCH

This study supports and adds an interesting new dimension to previous research on how hard students work to complete tasks and how effectively they learn whilst completing them. Previous studies have found that many students tend to procrastinate, though their performance and efficiency is improved if they have deadlines to work towards (#56).

Part of this procrastination is due to students under-estimating how long a task will take to complete (#3). Providing feedback on how long is left in the task can help combat this. Research suggests that once we know the end is near, we tend to accelerate our behaviour. As the authors of the study noted, "it has been found that the rate at which consumers buy coffee increases the closer to finishing a stamp card and receiving free coffee" and also that "runners increase speed closer to a finish line".

Another potential reason why the students in this study performed better if they knew how long was left in the task was due to the fog of uncertainty being lifted. This freed them up to focus more on the task at hand. Other research has found a strong link between uncertainty and stress (#60). It appears that providing updates gives clarity which enhances both motivation and mood.

CLASSROOM IMPLICATIONS

Teachers can apply the findings of this study very simply and effectively. The authors suggest how the "effects of boredom, and perhaps even disengagement, can be countervailed using a simple procedure of providing individuals information on their distance from the finish line. In applied contexts (e.g. classrooms, work) mentioning to students how many more problems are left to solve or informing workers how close they are to end of a shift can have beneficial outcomes for performance as well as for affect and well-being".

THE ONE ABOUT INTERLEAVING AND DISCRIMINATION LEARNING

@inner_drive | www.innerdrive.co.uk

THE STUDY

Students often have to learn similar-sounding yet very distinct concepts. For example, in Biology, students have to learn about "transcription, transduction, transformation and translation – four terms with similar spellings and meanings". Students often struggle with this. Being able to distinguish between similar sounding concepts is known as "discrimination learning".

Interleaving has been found to enhance learning and memory; it is the process of mixing up the order of topics that students learn, so as to help them make connections and choose the best strategy when solving a different problem (the opposite being "blocking", which is covering one topic exclusively at a time). So, could interleaving help aid students to distinguish between their learning of similar concepts better? Researchers carried out a review of the existing literature to find out.

BLOCKING TOPIC 1 › TOPIC 2 › TOPIC 3 › TOPIC 4

INTERLEAVING

TOPIC 1 TOPIC 2 TOPIC 3 TOPIC 4 › TOPIC 2 TOPIC 1 TOPIC 3 TOPIC 4 › TOPIC 3 TOPIC 4 TOPIC 1 TOPIC 2 › TOPIC 3 TOPIC 4 TOPIC 1 TOPIC 2

THE MAIN FINDINGS

Interleaving was found to:

1 Help students **improve their discrimination** learning. This is because with blocked practice "students need not identify an appropriate strategy because every problem in the assignment can be solved by the same strategy".

2 Help students **perform better** in final exams.

3 Work in a **range of subjects** – maths, art and sport were **specifically highlighted**.

4 Be **beneficial for a large age range of students** from primary through to university students.

Ref: Rohrer, 2012, Educational Psychology Review.

THE ONE ABOUT INTERLEAVING AND DISCRIMINATION LEARNING

 ## RELATED RESEARCH

Research suggests that the interleaving practice is effective in helping students to improve their learning (#1). This study helps to highlight the mechanism involved. Other studies support the long-term nature of this effect, with one in particular finding that, when students were given a surprise test a month after learning the study material, those that interleaved their learning outscored the blocked group by almost double.

Not only is interleaving useful in academics, but the positive effects of it can also be seen in other fields, such as sport. For example, research shows that when PE students had to learn three different types of badminton serves, those in the interleaved group who practiced the serves in a random order performed better later on than those in the blocked group.

CLASSROOM IMPLICATIONS

Interleaving is beneficial to students for many reasons, meaning that its popularity in education is justified. But, as with any new and exciting concept, it can be misunderstood. This means that several interleaving myths exist. One such myth is that interleaving is the same as spacing (#4). Spacing concerns time and is the idea that revisiting the same material often is more effective than studying it one chunk. Interleaving, on the other hand, is about mixing up the order of topics. This of course means not only that there is an element of spacing to interleaving but also that not all spacing is interleaving.

Another misconception around interleaving is that it involves mixing up subjects as well as topics. Interleaving is effective, as it helps students to make connections between related concepts, helps them to focus harder on choosing an appropriate strategy or both. This means that unrelated subjects may not get a benefit from interleaving.

The final misconception about interleaving is that it is a quick win. Research (#15) has found that if students were tested on the same day that they had learnt the material, their performance was much better if they had blocked their studying. However, when students were tested on their abilities one week later, performance in the interleaved condition was vastly superior. Since many students are tested a month, a year or two years after first being taught something, this suggests that schools would do well to consider how they interleave their curriculum.

THE ONE ABOUT HOW TEACHERS GIVE FEEDBACK

@inner_drive | www.innerdrive.co.uk

THE STUDY

Feedback given at the right time and in the right way has the ability to transform students and accelerate their learning. Yet despite its importance and the amount of time spent on feedback, until fairly recently, little has been known about the ways that teachers actually deliver it.

Researchers recently explored when, how and why teachers give feedback. To assess this, the researchers posed hypothetical scenarios to teachers and got them to rate the likelihood of how they would respond. This was done based on whether the students had succeeded or failed at a task, how difficult the task was and on the teacher's own mindset.

THE MAIN FINDINGS

1 When Teachers Give Feedback

- Teachers were more likely to give feedback to students who **had been successful** compared to those who failed.

- Teachers were more likely to give feedback to the students who were doing a **particularly difficult task**.

2 Different Types of Feedback

- If students **were successful**, teachers were more likely to **use a combination** of 'person feedback' (i.e. 'you are so smart') and 'process feedback' (i.e. the strategy used to solve the task).

- If students **failed the task**, teachers were more likely to give **process feedback** on how the students could do the task better the next time.

3 Teacher Mindset and Feedback

- Teachers with a fixed mindset were more likely to give a **combination of person and process feedback** if students **were successful**. A teacher's mindset **made no difference** when it came to the type of feedback given if a student had **failed the task**.

Ref: Skipper and Douglas, 2019, British Journal of Educational Psychology.

THE ONE ABOUT HOW TEACHERS GIVE FEEDBACK

 ## RELATED RESEARCH

This study builds on previous research that demonstrated the powerful impact that teachers' comments have on their students (#64). Evidence suggests that feedback plays a significant role in a student's learning, emotions and student satisfaction. Yet with this great power comes great responsibility, as evidence has shown that, if misused, feedback can cause more harm than good (#25). It is interesting that this study found that teachers were more likely to use "process" feedback if students had failed at a task, as one of the largest-ever reviews into feedback suggests that this type of feedback often leads to deeper learning.

Finally, the finding that teacher mindset affected the type of feedback the teachers provided if the students were successful but not if they failed supports existing research and extends our understanding on the many and subtle ways mindset influences students' thoughts and feelings. Previous research (#7) has demonstrated that a teacher's mindset impacts how likely they are to focus on comfort-focused feedback (i.e. making people feel good) or strategy-focused feedback (i.e. how to get better at the task).

CLASSROOM IMPLICATIONS

Because failure often represents a good potential learning opportunity, it is interesting to note that this study found that teachers are more likely to give feedback following a successful task than if students had failed. This is known as a "teachable moment" and is arguably when students need feedback the most. The key, however, is to try and find a balance as it is also true that success can often start a positive cycle of enhanced motivation which leads to further success.

As well as the "when", the type of feedback that teachers give is also worth deep consideration. Focusing on "person feedback" may help build self-esteem in the short term, but in the long term it is unlikely to yield the same level of learning that process feedback does. The latter, however, with its many known benefits, is likely to take more time and requires more personalisation, which is something teachers will have to weigh on a case-by-case basis.

THE ONE ABOUT THE PEAK END EFFECT

@inner_drive | www.innerdrive.co.uk

THE STUDY

Ever noticed how pop stars save their best song until last at a gig? This is because they want you to have the best time right at the end, so that you leave thinking the whole concert was great. This is an example of the Peak End Effect, in which people remember and place more weight on the end of an experience than on the experience as a whole.

This psychological quirk was first studied in the early 1990s by pioneering psychologist Daniel Kahneman and his colleagues, in a fascinating study. The researchers subjected their participants to two unpleasant experiences. In part one, they had each individual place their hands in 14°C water for one minute. In part two, the participants had to again place their hand in 14°C water for one minute and then in 15°C water for an additional 30 seconds. After both of these experiences, the participants then had to choose which of the two experiences they wanted to repeat. Would they choose 60 seconds of a lot of unpleasantness, or 60 seconds of a lot of unpleasantness followed by 30 seconds of a bit of discomfort?

THE MAIN FINDINGS

1 69% of participants **chose to repeat the longer trial**. The researchers note that "this proportion would be zero if subjects acted to **minimize their exposure to pain**". Additional tests showed that "choices did not depend on whether the long trial was experienced first or second or with the dominant or nondominant hand".

2 The participants **who found the slightly warmer water** in the second trial much less unpleasant were **far more likely** to repeat the longer trial.

3 Most of the subjects stated that **the longer trial caused less overall discomfort**, was less tough to cope with and less cold at its most extreme moment.
But as the researchers reflected, "the long trial contained all the pain of the short trial and then some, these post-choice judgements are simply wrong". This means that participants chose to repeat the trial they **remembered as being easiest**, even if it wasn't. This is because they placed too much weight on the last 30 seconds of the trial.

Ref: Kahneman et al, 1993. Association for Psychological Science.

THE ONE ABOUT THE PEAK END EFFECT

RELATED RESEARCH

This seminal study helped changed the way psychologists (and indeed economists and many other professionals including teachers) view human behaviour, as it has profound impacts on how we make decisions. In this case, by ending on a high – or technically a not as bad of a low – it altered how people remembered the event. This confirms that people have a subjective perception of both time and their experiences (#27). Other cognitive biases that have since been discovered include "anchoring" (i.e. where an initial number/piece of information weighs heavily in one's mind) and "framing" (i.e. if the options are presented in either a positive or negative light).

One study on anchoring found that people who were asked to estimate the total of the calculation 1x2x3x4x5x6x7x8, guessed a much lower total (average guess was 512) than those who were presented with the calculation written as 8x7x6x5x4x3x2x1 (average guess was 2,250). This is because, in the latter version, the numbers were higher at the beginning and as such were anchored in the participants' minds.

In a study on framing, people were asked to make medical decisions based on whether there was a 90% survival rate versus a 10% chance of dying. Even though this was the same probability, the different numbers led to very different decisions being made. Likewise, a different study on students found that 93% of them registered early for a course when a fine for being late was highlighted, yet only 63% did so if they were told they would receive a discount for registering early.

CLASSROOM IMPLICATIONS

This study can be used by teachers, as it suggests that the end of the lesson will affect how students will feel about the lesson as a whole. This can be useful when it comes to motivating bored students (#26), dealing with times when they are likely to get distracted (#48) and improving the likelihood of them not forgetting key pieces of information (#66). Just as pop stars play their best songs to finish a concert, it would probably be a wise idea for teachers to end their lessons on a high note to help students develop positive associations towards their subject, lesson and teacher.

THE ONE ABOUT THE IMPORTANCE OF FAILING

@inner_drive | www.innerdrive.co.uk

THE STUDY

The researchers of this paper opened with the brilliant quote by Nobel prize winner Robert Lefkowitz who said, "Science is 99% failure, and that's an optimistic view". So, as well as being somewhat inevitable, is failure also essential?

To test this, researchers from Universities in China and America recently tracked early career scientists applying for national grants. They compared those who had failed to win a grant by a small margin (labelled 'near-misses') with those who had just obtained the required threshold (labelled 'near wins').

THE MAIN FINDINGS

1 **10%** of these early career scientists who experienced a 'near-miss' **were highly demotivated** and this led to them not applying for research grants again.

2 Those who experienced a **'near-miss' early in their career**, had a similar number of research papers published over the **next 10 years** to those who had experienced a 'near win' at the beginning of their career.

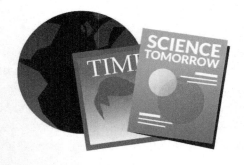

3 Fascinatingly, when looking at **who had published** a 'hit' paper in the subsequent five years (which was defined as being in the top **5%** of cited papers), the 'near-miss' scientists, were over **20% more likely to have published a 'hit' paper**, compared to the 'near winners'.

4 The researchers also found that the 'near misses' were **more likely to have had their work cited by other scientists** and there was more potential to have their work translated into other languages. The researchers say these results show that the mantra of "what doesn't kill you **makes you stronger**" may indeed be true.

Ref: Wang et al, 2019. Nature Communications.

THE ONE ABOUT THE IMPORTANCE OF FAILING

 ## RELATED RESEARCH

The main finding that early failures may help budding scientists is an interesting one, given that previous research (#74) has indicated that if students hear about scientists who have failed at some stage in their career, then they feel more connected to them. Subsequently, this led to students achieving higher grades in their science exams (with this impact felt most strongly by students who had previously been struggling). One possible mechanism that causes this, that coming to the realisation that failure need not be fatal, may help invoke and inspire a growth mindset, which has been shown to help resilience, self-esteem and enjoyment in the task itself (#5, #68).

Previous research on the effect of success and failure has shown a large range of findings. Some studies have shown a Matthew Effect (i.e. in which the rich get richer), as early success can help fuel future successes because of enhanced recognition, confidence, motivation and resources. On the other hand, other studies have shown the potential benefits of failure, which include learning from the experience, boosted motivation, developing resilience and increasing compassion.

CLASSROOM IMPLICATIONS

The researchers flag a clear warning that, despite the powerful effect that early failure can have on the likelihood of one's future success, "one should not put roadblocks in the way of junior scientists, as the precondition of becoming stronger is not to be killed in the first place". Essentially, failure is a double-edged sword - it can both help and hinder, so it would be a mistake to artificially manufacture it too much.

Instead, they suggest that their findings should be taken as a sign of comfort for those who do struggle, as "for those who persevere, early failure should not be taken as a negative signal" - rather, it should be taken as the opposite, in line with Shinya Yamanaka's advice to young scientists after he won the Nobel prize for the discovery of iPS cells: "I can see any failure as a chance".

Tips

Tips for improving memory

So what can you do if you really want to make learning stick? Evidence suggests that the following strategies offer the best bang for your buck:

- ✓ **Retrieval practice** – This is any activity that forces students to come up with answers.

- ✓ **Space out learning** – Doing little and often is better than doing a lot all at once.

- ✓ **Interleaving** – Varying the type of problems students answer within a topic.

- ✓ **Pre-questions** – Ask questions about the material before teaching it.

- ✓ **Elaborative interrogation** – Getting students to ask "why is this the case?" or "why is this true for X but not for Y?".

- ✓ **Dual coding** – Combine pictures and words – this utilises dual coding and the Production Effect and reduces chances of cognitive overload.

- ✓ **Don't listen to music** – (Especially those with lyrics) when learning new or complex material. It really won't help.

- ✓ **Don't simply re-read the material or just highlight key passages** – These activities can be done on autopilot, which does not lead to deep and lasting learning.

- ✓ **Teach the material to someone else** – This helps students learn the material more deeply and organises their knowledge.

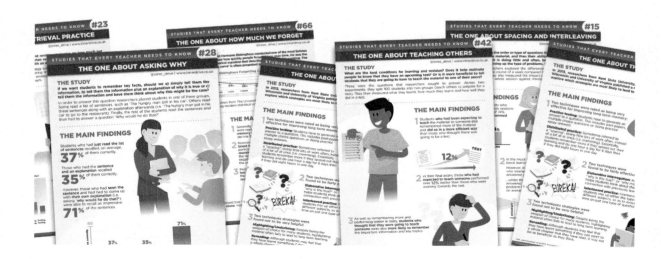

Tips for improving mindset, motivation and resilience

To help encourage a learning mindset and to prompt high levels of effort and persistence:

✔ **Help students believe that they can improve and get better.** This can be done by focusing on:
- Effort and study strategies instead of natural ability
- Processes as well as the outcome
- Viewing mistakes as feedback and as an opportunity to learn

✔ **Developing a sense of purpose** – Help students connect their current activity with how it will help them achieve their future goals.

✔ **Explaining failures** – Encourage students to not always internalise the causes of their failures, as this will reduce resilience.

✔ **Explaining successes** – Prompt students to reflect on their success. If they attribute it to external factors or luck, this will chip away at both their motivation and confidence.

✔ **Seek out support** – Encourage students to use the support available to them. Help them see that asking for help is a sign of strength, not of weakness.

✔ **Control the controllables** – Remind students to focus on what is important and what is within their control.

✔ **Challenge and support** – For resilience to thrive, an environment must be both demanding and supportive.

✔ **Embrace Failure** – This can help boost motivation, learning and resilience.

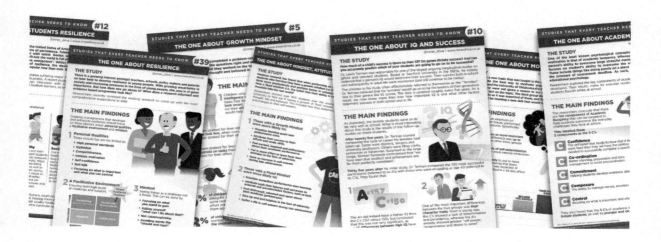

Tips for improving self-regulation and metacognition

Having high self-awareness and the ability to choose helpful thought processes and strategies is the bedrock of learning. This can be maximised by:

- ✓ **Getting plenty of sleep** – Teenagers and adolescents need it more than adults. Aim for 8–10 hours.

- ✓ **Controlling the inner narrative** – How students talk to themselves will impact how they think, feel and behave.

- ✓ **Managing mobile phones** – Students who don't have them around concentrate more and learn more efficiently.

- ✓ **Improve self-reflection** – Encourage students to ask themselves:
  - Which resources will help me study?
  - Why is this resource helpful?
  - How will I use this resource?

- ✓ **Delayed gratification** – Sometimes it is better to suffer in the short term in order to prosper in the long term.

- ✓ **Distractions** – Students are more likely to be distracted on Mondays and Fridays; plan accordingly.

- ✓ **Don't say don't** – It is better for students to focus on what they do want and not on what they don't want.

- ✓ **Not all stress is bad** – Stress is often driven by uncertainty, but not all stress is bad. If students focus on how it will help them then it will boost performance.

- ✓ **Develop metacognitive skills** – Teach these across the whole curriculum, not just in discrete one-off lessons.

Tips for students

Actions speak louder than words. There is little point in having good intentions if you do not convert them into positive behaviours. Here are some simple strategies that you can start implementing straight away that will lead to better learning:

✓ **Eat breakfast** – It is one of the easiest ways to boost mood, memory and grades.

✓ **Take notes during class.** To do this effectively:
  • Use pen and paper instead of laptops
  • Don't write everything down word for word, summarise it in your own words
  • Make notes at the end of each section or topic

✓ **Have high aspirations and expectations** of yourself whilst at school.

✓ **Choose study mates carefully;** effort is contagious.

✓ **Turn down the backlight** on mobile phones a few hours before bed – it will help you sleep much better.

✓ **Don't spend too long daydreaming about the perfect future** – It can distract you and lead to procrastination. If you visualise things about the future, picture yourself doing the behaviours that will actually lead to that success.

✓ **Manage screen time** – Excessive screen time may make you think and feel worse.

Tips for teachers' attitudes, expectations and behaviours

Teachers play a crucial role in how much students learn. Evidence suggests that the following classroom practices will prompt a deeper level of learning and accelerate student development:

✓ **Have high expectations for all your students** – This means believing that every one of them can improve and develop their abilities.

✓ **Focus on strategy** – When students don't do well, focus on strategy as well as just making them feel better about their situation.

✓ **Don't aim to be liked** - Teacher popularity is not linked to how much students learn from that teacher. Instead, focus on building trust.

✓ **Use feedback wisely** – Feedback is a double-edged sword. Some feedback does more harm than good. Specifically, know that:

- Feedback that comments on the student's ability level is usually less effective than that which focuses on how to do the task better next time.
- Feedback that aims to improve motivation can improve subsequent efforts, but if students become reliant on it, then their performance can suffer if it is withdrawn.

✓ **Set homework regularly** – However, when students do more than 90 minutes a night, they gain little further advantage.

✓ **Choose classroom decorations carefully + selectively** – Too much may actually hinder learning.

✓ **Develop expertise** – This can be done by asking for help and advice from colleagues.

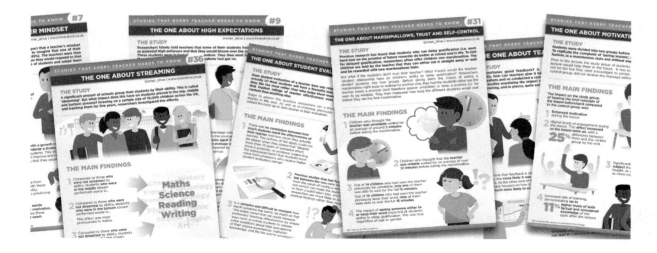

Tips for parents

Parents want the best for their child. The following hit-list provides a strong foundation to support your child's learning and development:

✔ **Have high academic expectations for your children.**
No-one rises to low expectations, and research suggests that this is the most important thing parents can do to help boost their child's academic achievement.

✔ **Read with your children** and do so regularly from a young age.

✔ **Respond well to failures and mistakes** by taking time to discuss how these are learning moments. Your children will be more likely to develop a growth mindset.

✔ **Don't overpraise.** It conveys low expectations and if done in comparison to other children can lead to your child developing narcissistic behaviour.

✔ **When you praise, focus on their processes and behaviours,** instead of the outcome or their natural abilities.

✔ **Eat dinner together with your child regularly** when possible; it offers invaluable time together to discuss how school is going.

✔ **Have a clear structure and rules** around how your child divides their homework and leisure time. Taking the time to explain the thought process behind these rules will also help.

✔ **Be involved.** Parental involvement is positively associated with student achievement, student self-perception and teacher-student relationships.

✔ **Know how much they sleep.** Getting enough sleep is so important for developing adolescent minds.

Tips for overcoming thinking biases

We are all less rational and logical than we would like to think. The truth is, there are lots of thinking biases that get in the way of learning. To avoid some of the pitfalls, here is what you need to know:

✓ **You have less time to complete a task than you think** – So plan properly and start early.

✓ **Don't be seduced by natural talent** – We are poor predictors of what future talent may look like. Therefore, don't always fall for the allure of the present and try to imagine alternative future scenarios.

✓ **Better self-awareness** – We are more likely to criticise our past selves than our current one. This is a short term self-protecting mechanism that can get in the way of accurately assessing our abilities and ideas.

✓ **Use objective data** – The lower our abilities are, the less accurately we are able to predict our current levels. Facts and stats are good ways to overcome this.

✓ **Don't fall for the spotlight effect** – People are often paying you far less attention than you think.

✓ **Don't fall in love with your own ideas** – We prefer our own ideas much more than those that someone else came up with it. This makes it harder to take criticism or to know when to change approach.

✓ **Don't always follow the crowd** – This leads to people sometimes making bad decisions or doing things they wouldn't usually do.

✓ **Be a bit sceptical** – Don't fall for fancy explanations about the brain or learning styles. Always ask for the evidence.

✓ **Know how long is left in the task** – This can boost motivation, learning and effort.

✓ **Finish on a positive** – We tend to remember the last thing we experienced.

When the science of learning meets the art of teaching

When the Science of Learning Meets the Art of Teaching

Knowing the research is one thing, but applying it is another. How you translate some of the research that this book covers into action will depend on your students, your subject and your context. So to help with this, we have taken one topic from each category and have looked in more detail into practical ways of implementing it, along with some of the potential obstacles and challenges that you may have to overcome along the way.

The topics we have taken from each category are:

Memory
Utilising retrieval practice in the classroom.

Mindset, Motivation and Resilience
Creating a growth culture.

Self-Regulation and Metacognition
Developing independent learners.

Student Behaviours
Managing mobile phones (and electronics in general).

Teacher Attitudes, Expectations and Behaviours
Mastering your classroom.

Parents
A home environment that aids learning.

Thinking Biases
Improving self-awareness through self-reflection.

@inner_drive | www.innerdrive.co.uk

RETRIEVAL PRACTICE

Retrieval practice (requiring students to generate an answer to a question) has been proven to be one of the most - if not the most - effective learning strategies. This is because requiring students to recall previously learnt knowledge creates stronger memory traces. This helps secure and embed information into students' long-term memory.

As such, retrieval practice warrants further attention and discussion. Specifically, the different ways a teacher can implement it and potential barriers to navigate whilst doing so.

HOW TO APPLY IT

There is no one set way of applying retrieval practice. It can take many forms, as long as at its core we are prompting students to search and recall what they know. Therefore, this can include:

- **PAST PAPERS** – these come with an added advantage of coming with feedback in the form of the answer scheme.

- **MULTIPLE CHOICE TESTS** – the fact that students can mark their own tests gives the advantages of retrieval practice without the addition of more teacher workload.

- **ESSAY ANSWERS** – avoids shallow learning as it helps teachers to see 'under the bonnet' by ensuring students aren't just regurgitating facts.

- **VERBAL Q&A** – this is quick to do, allows us to check their level of understanding and can be quite fun too.

- **FLASHCARDS** – a popular revision tool, just be sure to remind students to spend more time recalling the answers instead of writing the questions.

One of the main challenges in ensuring retrieval practice is effective is not to reduce it to a tick box exercise. Different types of questions and different formats should help. It also shouldn't be confused with doing more tests, because 'tests' can bring about fears of being judged and worry about the implications of failing.

It is better to think about retrieval practice as quizzes, rather than exams. This means doing it in a relatively stress free manner and in a way that focuses on recalling what they know and not on how they rank relative to their peers.

@inner_drive | www.innerdrive.co.uk

CREATING A GROWTH CULTURE

Growth mindset, grit, resilience: it's been called many things by educators and researchers alike. And though there are important distinctions between the three, in a practical sense they all boil down to the same thing; we want students who believe they can get better and who are motivated to keep going in the face of setbacks.

To help develop this in our students, it is best to think of it more as a philosophy rather than an intervention. It's not a one-off assembly or a motivational poster. It is more about creating a culture of excellence, where we set the right environment that helps students to want to work hard, learn and improve. So, what does a growth culture look like?

HOW TO APPLY IT

At its core, a growth culture is about maintaining motivation to help students develop. This can be achieved in several ways. Firstly, by **encouraging students to compare themselves to themselves**. Many will naturally compare themselves to others, as a way of working out where they fit into the pecking order of things. Short term, this may boost performance, but long term it is not a very robust strategy for motivation and is associated with slower rates of learning and enhanced stress.

Secondly, **the environment needs to be one of high expectations**, both of what we think they can achieve but also of what **they** think they can achieve. Once expectations are lowered, excuses and 'the blame game' become more prevalent, which can ultimately stunt growth.

Finally, it's about **creating an environment that treads the line between celebrating success without resting on their laurels**, whilst also learning from mistakes without dwelling on them. This can feel like a fine line to tread. When they inevitably don't get the balance quite right, they should be kind to themselves and move on. Tomorrow is always another day to go again.

One potential challenge when it comes to developing a growth culture is that it can sometimes feel quite abstract. It can be hard to describe, and yet you know it when you see it. Within this ambiguity, consistency across a whole school can be tricky. That's why a good starting place is to have an agreed set of values that underpins your school culture. If you have that foundation, then individual decisions along the way are easier to make, as they can be related back to those core values.

@inner_drive | www.innerdrive.co.uk

DEVELOPING INDEPENDENT LEARNERS

One of the aims in education is to help our students become independent learners. This arguably becomes increasingly important as they progress through school. In order to do this effectively, they need to be able to manage their motivation, thoughts, and emotions.

To build up their ability to do this, the strategy of "scaffolding" is helpful. Similar to the scaffolding used in construction, it entails teachers creating a support structure in place, and then reducing the amount incrementally as the student progresses.

HOW TO APPLY IT

One of the main issues is how difficult it is to know how much scaffolding we offer students at different times in their journey towards full independent learning. This is because **a) learning is not linear** (which means that the amount of support we may need to offer can vary from one day to the next) and **b) some failure is probably good for them long term**. Though it may be hard to see them struggle with a task and therefore tempting to jump in to help them, the only way to know and improve their current level is for them to stretch themselves at times.

Evidence suggests that **decreasing support too quickly can do more harm than good**. If it is rushed, then a student's anxiety, stress and self-limiting perceptions of their abilities may be affected. For it to be effective, scaffolding needs to be both well thought out and gradually reduced.

Scaffolding isn't just about technical support. To help students develop as independent learners, we need to scaffold the emotional support as well. This means **teaching them how to manage their thoughts and feelings**. For example, helping them develop skills such as how they talk to themselves and what they actively focus on will help. Although these skills can develop naturally, they can also be accelerated if we explicitly talk to students about them.

One of the main challenges in developing this area of learning is that there is sometimes a false dichotomy created between pastoral and academic interventions. This makes it sound like it is either-or. However, the truth is that the two are not mutually exclusive. Interventions that target helping students develop their response to stress, setbacks and frustrations can help aid both.

@inner_drive | www.innerdrive.co.uk

MANAGING MOBILE PHONES (AND ELECTRONICS IN GENERAL)

Arguably one of the biggest question educators face in the 21st century is: to what extent should they introduce electronic technology into their classrooms? The call for it is high, both from students who love their mobile phones and from parents who want their children to utilise modern technology.

Without doubt, electronics offer a range of learning opportunities – from searching for information, to sharing ideas, to capturing what was discussed to checking levels of student understanding via instant quizzes. However, left unchecked or without forethought on the potential downsides, electronics can do more harm than good. These include reduced concentration, memory, learning and overall academic performance. So what can teachers do to maximise the upsides and mitigate the downsides?

HOW TO APPLY IT

When deciding how or if you want to introduce electronics into your classroom, it is worth starting with the problem that you are trying to solve, and not with what the technology offers. Focusing on the question prompts you to focus on what solutions would work best for you. **Doing it the wrong way round** by starting with the seduction of the technology can unfortunately lead you down a path where you try to shoe-horn the technology into the lesson for the sake of it. Just because an app, website or mobile phone/website has the capacity to do something does not mean it has to be included. If it doesn't aid student learning, then it is nothing more than expensive window dressing.

Likewise, it is worth considering the opportunity cost of using mobile phones within a lesson. Does its benefit outweigh the cost/time/potential distractions that might come with it? **It is not necessarily a straightforward question as to whether mobile phones/tablets are better than pen and paper**, but are they better enough to justify it.

One way to help do this is to consider everything that could go wrong. This will include devices running out of battery, students forgetting to bring them with them for that lesson, WiFi connectivity issues and students using them for different purposes than you intended. Considering a back-up or alternative plan is prudent event planning, and can help a) the decision as to whether to use electronics and b) make how to do so a lot smoother.

THIS IS WHERE THE SCIENCE OF LEARNING...

...MEETS THE ART OF TEACHING

@inner_drive | www.innerdrive.co.uk

MASTERING YOUR CLASSROOM

There is a lovely saying: "teaching is the one profession that creates all the other professions". Developing teaching expertise is therefore both a moral and personal imperative. But how does one go about this? Subject knowledge is clearly important, but there is a lot more that makes great teaching. We think that building positive teacher-student relationships and having an up to date understanding of research are two good ways to improve one's expertise.

HOW TO APPLY IT

Developing positive teacher-student relationships is a big part of being able to master your classroom. This can be built through a combination of setting the bar high and consistency. **Consistency helps build trust**, which is the hallmark of a reliable classroom. Likewise, **setting a high bar in terms of behaviour**, which have been clearly communicated and regularly enforced, creates an optimal learning environment.

One of the challenges is not to fall into the trap of confusing positive teacher-student relationships with being popular amongst students. Instead, it is more about **setting high standards in a warm and fair way**. As a result, students may not always like or agree with what you say, but they will know that you are doing it with their best interests at heart.

With so much great information out there in the form of research studies, education books and blogs, accessing brilliant personal CPD has never been easier. **The more you read, the more it can help both challenge and confirm some of your previously held beliefs**. This can help you view your own experience through a different lens. Whatever the topic, be it behaviour management, curriculum design, how to measure learning or giving feedback, someone somewhere has written about it.

This can also be supplemented by **asking lots of questions of your colleagues and asking for help if need** be. It is interesting to reflect how a recent study found that one of the hallmarks of expert teachers is that they are more likely to seek feedback from their peers. This suggests that the hunger to learn about our own craft is one of the best ways to improve it.

@inner_drive | www.innerdrive.co.uk

A HOME ENVIRONMENT THAT AIDS LEARNING

The difficulty for many parents is that they are well positioned to give advice and support to their children, and yet for many, when their child enters their teenage years especially, they are the last person students want to take advice from. This is a classic case of it being about the messenger, not the message. Therefore, the closer schools and parents can work together, to ensure they are providing a consistent message, the more likely students are to take heed of the advice.

The challenge for schools is that they do not have as much influence in this domain as they do in their classroom. So, how can schools educate the parents on how they can best support their child's learning?

HOW TO APPLY IT

One of the key themes that emerges from the research on parental behaviour is the concept of **"little and often"** as opposed to one-off big conversations infrequently. This allows emerging issues to be addressed whilst they are only bubbling away and not only when they are reaching explosion levels. Having dinner and reading together provide good opportunities for this.

Another interesting finding is how **"more isn't always better"**. So for example, students did better long term when parents didn't directly assist them with their homework. Those that did well were ones who had parents that put in place a clear structure and rules, but then gave them enough autonomy to work within that.

It also seems that if nothing else, having high academic expectations and really valuing the process of education and what teachers/schools are doing has a pronounced effect. It is very easy for our own story to be internalised by our children (a classic example being **"I wasn't good at maths when I was your age"**). This suggests we do not need to know the answer to all their questions about their school work, which is a common fear for many parents, but by valuing their child's efforts to find out and providing a system where they can go and learn the answer for themselves seems to be a wise approach.

@inner_drive | www.innerdrive.co.uk

IMPROVING SELF-AWARENESS THROUGH SELF-REFLECTION

Our thought processes are not always the clearest. They are not always the most rational. We all suffer from a number of thinking biases that can hinder how much and how quickly we learn. Frustratingly, one of these biases is the "Blindspot Bias", in which we think that other people suffer from these biases but fail to acknowledge our own biases.

This makes overcoming these biases very hard to do. Although they will always be present to some extent, we can help our students mitigate the impact they might have. One way that we can help both ourselves and our students overcome these biases is to improve our self-awareness through better self-reflection.

HOW TO APPLY IT

There are several strategies that can help students overcome common thinking biases. One strategy is to use objective data. **Opinions can be subjective, but data leaves less wiggle room for interpretation.** For example, if students think they are doing better than they actually are (the Dunning-Kruger effect), then the challenge when presenting information about their current level is to help them realise the reality of the situation whilst understanding it can be improved if they make changes to how they are studying.

The best time to improve self-reflection is to discuss things when both they and you are not too emotional. If emotions run too high, then this leads to a counterproductive situation of **"more heat than light"**. The noise of the emotions can deafen them to the strategies and solutions you are proposing.

One of the big obstacles with helping students develop their self-awareness is time. In an already crowded timetable, carving out time to discuss this sort of thing can be tricky, especially as each student has their own unique personality and thinking biases. **Improving self-awareness through self-reflection is not a quick or an easy win**. It is worth it, as it can act as a multiplier, as the benefit of doing so is felt across all the subjects they study and across all domains of their lives.

REFERENCE LIST: THE STUDIES

1. Dunlosky, J., Rawson, K. A., Marsh, E. J., Nathan, M. J., & Willingham, D. T. (2013). Improving students' learning with effective learning techniques: Promising directions from cognitive and educational psychology. *Psychological Science in the Public Interest, 14*(1), 4-58.

2. Khattab, N. (2015). Students' aspirations, expectations and school achievement: What really matters? *British Educational Research Journal, 41*(5), 731-748.

3. Buehler, R., Griffin, D., & Ross, M. (1994). Exploring the "planning fallacy": Why people underestimate their task completion times. *Journal of Personality and Social Psychology, 67*(3), 366.

4. Cepeda, N. J., Vul, E., Rohrer, D., Wixted, J. T., & Pashler, H. (2008). Spacing effects in learning a temporal ridgeline of optimal retention. *Psychological Science, 19*(11), 1095-1102.

5. Mueller, C. M., & Dweck, C. S. (1998). Praise for intelligence can undermine children's motivation and performance. *Journal of Personality and Social Psychology, 75*(1), 33.

6. Epley, N., & Dunning, D. (2000). Feeling "holier than thou": Are self-serving assessments produced by errors in self-or social prediction? *Journal of Personality and Social Psychology, 79*(6), 861.

7. Rattan, A., Good, C., & Dweck, C. S. (2012). "It's ok: Not everyone can be good at math": Instructors with an entity theory comfort (and demotivate) students. *Journal of Experimental Social Psychology, 48*(3), 731-737.

8. Sebastian, C., Viding, E., Williams, K. D., & Blakemore, S. J. (2010). Social brain development and the affective consequences of ostracism in adolescence. *Brain and Cognition, 72*(1), 134-145.

9. Rosenthal, R., & Jacobson, L. (1968). Pygmalion in the classroom. *The Urban Review, 3*(1), 16-20.

10. Terman, L. M., & Oden, M. H. (1959). *The gifted group at mid-life: Thirty-five years follow-up of a superior group.* Stanford, CA: Stanford University Press.

11. Castro, M., Expósito-Casas, E., López-Martín, E., Lizasoain, L., Navarro-Asencio, E., & Gaviria, J. L. (2015). Parental involvement on student academic achievement: A meta-analysis. *Educational Research Review, 14*, 33-46.

12. Holdsworth, S., Turner, M., & Scott-Young, C. M. (2017). . . . Not drowning, waving: Resilience and university: A student perspective. *Studies in Higher Education,* 1-17.

13. Shoda, Y., Mischel, W., & Peake, P. K. (1990). Predicting adolescent cognitive and self-regulatory competencies from preschool delay of gratification: Identifying diagnostic conditions. *Developmental Psychology, 26*(6), 978.

14. Paunesku, D., Walton, G. M., Romero, C., Smith, E. N., Yeager, D. S., & Dweck, C. S. (2015). Mind-set interventions are a scalable treatment for academic underachievement. *Psychological Science, 26*(6), 1-10.

15. Rohrer, D., & Taylor, K. (2007). The shuffling of mathematics problems improves learning. *Instructional Science, 35*, 481-498.

16. Haimovitz, K., & Dweck, C. (2016). What predicts children's fixed and growth mind-sets? Not their parents' view of intelligence but their parents' views of failure. *Psychological Science, 27*(6), 859-869.

17. Perham, N., & Currie, H. (2014). Does listening to preferred music improve reading comprehension performance? *Applied Cognitive Psychology, 28*(2), 279-284.

18. Kruger, J., & Dunning, D. (1999). Unskilled and unaware of it: How difficulties in recognizing one's own incompetence lead to inflated self-assessments. *Journal of Personality and Social Psychology, 77*(6), 1121.

19. Gunderson, E., Gripshover, S., Romero, C., Dweck, C., Goldin-Meadow, S., & Levine, S. (2013). Parental praise to 1-3 year olds precits children's motivation framework 5 years later on. *Child Development,* 1-16.

20. Desender, K., Beurms, S., & Van den Bussche, E. (2016). Is mental effort exertion contagious? *Psychonomic Bulletin & Review, 23*(2), 624-631.

21. Uttl, B., White, C. A., & Gonzalez, D. W. (2016). Meta-analysis of faculty's teaching effectiveness: Student evaluation of teaching ratings and student learning are not related. *Studies in Educational Evaluation, 54,* 22-42.

22. Tsay, C. J., & Banaji, M. R. (2011). Naturals and strivers: Preferences and beliefs about sources of achievement. *Journal of Experimental Social Psychology, 47*(2), 460-465.

23. Roediger III, H. L., & Karpicke, J. D. (2006). Test-enhanced learning: Taking memory tests improves long-term retention. *Psychological Science, 17*(3), 249-255.

24. Wegner, D., Schneider, D., Carter, S., & White, T. (1987). Paradoxical effects of though suppression. *Journal of Personality and Social Psychology, 53*(1), 5-13.

25. Kluger, A., & DeNisi, A. (1996). The effects of feedback interventions on performance: A historical review, a meta-analysis and a preliminary feedback intervention theory. *Psychological Bulletin, 119*(2), 254-284.

26. Jang, H. (2008). Supporting students' motivation, engagement, and learning during an uninteresting activity. *Journal of Educational Psychology, 100*(4), 798.

27. Wilson, A., & Ross, M. (2001). From chump to champ: People's appraisals of their earlier and present selves. *Journal of Personality and Social Psychology, 80*(4), 572-584.

28. Pressley, M., McDaniel, M. A., Turnure, J. E., Wood, E., & Ahmad, M. (1987). Generation and precision of elaboration: Effects on intentional and incidental learning. *Journal of Experimental Psychology: Learning, Memory, and Cognition, 13*(2), 291.

29. Walker, M. P., & van Der Helm, E. (2009). Overnight therapy? The role of sleep in emotional brain processing. *Psychological Bulletin, 135*(5), 731.

30. Thornton, B., Faires, A., Robbins, M., & Rollins, E. (2014). The mere presence of a cell phone may be distracting. *Social Psychology, 45*(6), 479-488.

31. Kidd, C., Palmeri, H., & Aslin, R. N. (2013). Rational snacking: Young children's decision-making on the marshmallow task is moderated by beliefs about environmental reliability. *Cognition, 126*(1), 109-114.

32. Peper, R. J., & Mayer, R. E. (1986). Generative effects of note-taking during science lectures. *Journal of Educational Psychology, 78*(1), 34-38.

33. Vergauwe, J., Wille, B., Feys, M., De Fruyt, F., & Anseel, F. (2015). Fear of being exposed: The trait-relatedness of the impostor phenomenon and its relevance in the work context. *Journal of Business and Psychology, 30*(3), 565-581.

34. Forrin, N., & MacLeod, C. (2018). This time it's personal: The memory benefit of hearing oneself. *Memory, 26*(4), 574-579.

35. Wesnes, K. A., Pincock, C., Richardson, D., Helm, G., & Hails, S. (2003). Breakfast reduces declines in attention and memory over the morning in schoolchildren. *Appetite, 41*(3), 329-331.

36. Samantha Parsons, & Sue Hallam. (2014). The impact of streaming on attainment at age seven: Evidence from the Millennium Cohort Study. *Oxford Review of Education, 40*(5), 567-589.

37. Martin, A. J., Colmar, S. H., Davey, L. A., & Marsh, H. W. (2010). Longitudinal modelling of academic buoyancy and motivation: Do the 5Cs hold up over time? *British Journal of Educational Psychology, 80*(3), 473-496.

38. Gilovich, T., Medvec, V. H., & Savitsky, K. (2000). The spotlight effect in social judgment: An egocentric bias in estimates of the salience of one's own actions and appearance. *Journal of Personality and Social Psychology, 78*(2), 211.

39. Fletcher, D., & Sarkar, M. (2016). Mental fortitude training: An evidence-based approach to developing psychological resilience for sustained success. *Journal of Sport Psychology in Action, 7*(3), 135-157.

40. Wood, B., Rea, M. S., Plitnick, B., & Figueiro, M. G. (2013). Light level and duration of exposure determine the impact of self-luminous tablets on melatonin suppression. *Applied Ergonomics, 44*(2), 237-240.

41. Mayer, R. E., & Anderson, R. B. (1991). Animations need narrations: An experimental test of a dual-coding hypothesis. *Journal of Educational Psychology, 83*(4), 484-490.

42. Nestojko, J., Bui, D., Kornell, N., & Bjork, E. (2014). Expecting to teach enhances learning and organization of knowledge in free recall of text passages. *Memory and Cognition, 42*(7), 1038-1048.

43. Atir, S., Rosenzweig, E., & Dunning, D. (2015). When knowledge knows no bounds self-perceived expertise predicts claims of impossible knowledge. *Psychological Science, 26*(8), 1295-1303.

44. Kerr, N., & Hertel, G. (2011). The Kohler group motivation gain: How to motivate the "weak links" in a group. *Social and Personality Psychology Compass, 5*(1), 43-55.

45. Norton, M., Mochon, D., & Ariely, D. (2011). The "IKEA effect": When labor leads to love. *Harvard Business School*, 1-33.

46. Parson, J., Adler, T., & Kaczala, C. (1982). Socialization of achievement attitudes and beliefs: Parental influences. *Child Development, 53*(2), 310-321.

47. Reeve, J., Jang, H., Carrell, D., Jeon, S., & Barch, J. (2004). Enhancing students' engagement by increasing teachers' autonomy support. *Motivation and Emotion, 28*(2), 147-169.

48. Wammes, J., Boucher, P., Seli, P., Cheyne, J., & Smilek, D. (2016). Mind wandering during lectures I: Changes in rates across an entire semester. *Scholarship of Teaching and Learning in Psychology, 2*(1), 13-32.

49. Beland, L. P., & Murphy, R. (2015). *Communication: Technology, distraction & student performance*. Centre of Economic Performance.

50. Miller, C., & Krizan, Z. (2016). Walking facilitates positive affect (even when expecting the opposite). *Emotion, 16*(5), 775-785.

51. Crum, A., Salovey, P., & Achor, S. (2013). Rethinking stress: The role of mindsets in determining the stress response. *Journal of Personality and Social Psychology, 104*(4), 716-733.

52. Hattie, J., & Timperley, H. (2007). The power of feedback. *Review of Educational Research, 77*(1), 81-112.

53. Kross, E., Bruehlman-Senecal, E., Park, J., Burson, A., Dougherty, A., Shablack, H., Bremner, R., Moser, J., & Ayduk, O. (2014). Self-talk as a regulatory mechanism: How you do it matters. *Journal of Personality and Social Psychology, 106*(2), 304.

54. Senechal, M., & LeFevre, J. (2002). Parental involvement in the development of children's reading skill: A five-year longitudinal study. *Child Development, 73*(2), 445-460.

55. Weisberg, D. S., Keil, F. C., Goodstein, J., Rawson, E., & Gray, J. R. (2008). The seductive allure of neuroscience explanations. *Journal of Cognitive Neuroscience, 20*(3), 470-477.

56. Ariely, D., & Wertenbroch, K. (2002). Procrastination, deadlines, and performance: Self-control by pre-commitment. *Psychological Science, 13*(3), 219-224.

57. Zhao, L., Heyman, G., Chen, L., & Lee, K. (2017). Telling young children they have a reputation for being smart promotes cheating. *Developmental Science, 21*(3), e12585.

58. Pekrun, R., Lichtenfeld, S., Marsh, H., Murayama, K., & Goetz, T. (2017). Achievement emotions and academic performance: Longitudinal models of reciprocal effects. *Child Development, 88*(5), 1653-1670.

59. Berman, M. G., Jonides, J., & Kaplan, S. (2008). The cognitive benefits of interacting with nature. *Psychological Science, 19*(12), 1207-1212.

60. De Berker, A., Rutledge, R., Mathys, C., Marshall, L., Cross, G., Dolan, R., & Bestman, S. (2016). Computations of uncertainty mediate acute stress responses in humans. *Nature Communications, 7*, 10996.

61. Chen, P., Chavez, O., Ong, D., & Gunderson, B. (2017). Strategic resource use for learning: A self-administered intervention that guides self-reflection on effective resource use enhances academic performance. *Psychological Science, 28*(6), 774-785.

62. Agasisti, T. et al. (2018). *Academic resilience: What schools and countries do to help disadvantaged students succeed in PISA*. OECD Education Working Papers No. 167, OECD.

63. Pham, L., & Taylor, S. (1999). From thought to action: Effects of process-versus outcome-based mental simulations on performance. *Personality and Social Psychology Bulletin, 25*(2), 250-260.

64. Burnett, P. C. (1999). Children's self-talk and academic self-concepts: The impact of teachers' statements. *Educational Psychology in Practice, 15*(3), 195-200.

65. Brummelman, E., Thomaes, S., Nelemans, S., Orobio, B., Overbeek, G., & Bushman, B. (2015). Origins of narcissism in children. *Proceedings of the National Academy of Sciences, 112*(12), 3659-3662.

66. Murre, J. M., & Dros, J. (2015). Replication and analysis of Ebbinghaus' forgetting curve. *PLoS One, 10*(7), e0120644.

67. Fernández-Alonso, R., Suárez-Álvarez, J., & Muñiz, J. (2015). Adolescents' homework performance in mathematics and science: Personal factors and teaching practices. *Journal of Educational Psychology, 107*(4), 1075-1085.

68. Robins, R., & Pals, J. (2002). Implicit self-theories in the academic domain: Implications for goal orientation, attributions, affect, and self-esteem change. *Self and Identity, 1*(4), 313-336.

69. Carpenter, S., & Toftness, A. (2017). The effect of prequestions on learning from video presentations. *Journal of Applied Research in Memory and Cognition, 6*(1), 104-109.

70. Pashler, H., McDaniel, M., Rohrer, D., & Bjork, R. (2008). Learning styles concepts and evidence. *Psychological Science in the Public Interest, 9*(3), 105-119.

71. Fulker, J., Story, M., Mellin, A., Leffert, N., Neumark-Sztainer, D., & French, S. (2006). Family dinner meal frequency and adolescent development: Relationship with developmental assets and high-risk behaviours. *Journal of Adolescent Health, 39*(3), 337-345.

72. Mueller, P., & Oppenheimer, D. (2014). The pen is mightier than the keyboard: Advantages longhand over laptop note taking. *Psychological Science, 25*(6), 1159-1168.

73. Asch, S. E. (1951). Effects of group pressure upon the modification and distortion of judgments. In H. Guetzkow (Ed.), *Groups, leadership and men; research in human relations* (pp. 177-190). Oxford, England: Carnegie Press.

74. Lin-Siegler, X., Ahn, J. N., Chen, J., Fang, F.-F. A., & Luna-Lucero, M. (2016). Even Einstein struggled: Effects of learning about great scientists' struggles on high school students' motivation to learn science. *Journal of Educational Psychology, 108*(3), 314-328.

75. Duckworth, A., Quinn, P., & Seligman, M. (2009). Positive predictors of teacher effectiveness. *Journal of Positive Psychology, 4*(6), 540-547.

76. Smith, A. M., Floerke, V. A., & Thomas, A. K. (2016). Retrieval practice protects memory against acute stress. *Science, 354*(6315), 1046-1048.

77. Kardas, M., & O'Brien, E. (2018). Easier seen than done: Merely watching others perform can foster an illusion of skill acquisition. *Psychological Science, 29*(4), 521-536.

78. Moreno, R., & Mayer, R. E. (2000). A coherence effect in multimedia learning: The case for minimizing irrelevant sounds in the design of multimedia instructional messages. *Journal of Educational Psychology, 92*(1), 117.

79. Spillane, J. P., Shirrell, M., & Adhikari, S. (2018). Constructing "experts" among peers: Educational infrastructure, test data, and teachers' interactions about teaching. *Educational Evaluation and Policy Analysis, 40*(4), 586-612.

80. Vasilev, M. R., Kirkby, J. A., & Angele, B. (2018). Auditory distraction during reading: A Bayesian meta-analysis of a continuing controversy. *Perspectives on Psychological Science, 13*(5), 567-597.

81. Borman, G. D., Rozek, C. S., Pyne, J., & Hanselman, P. (2019). Reappraising academic and social adversity improves middle school students' academic achievement, behavior, and well-being. *Proceedings of the National Academy of Sciences, 116*(33), 16286-16291.

82. Schmeck, A., Mayer, R. E., Opfermann, M., Pfeiffer, V., & Leutner, D. (2014). Drawing pictures during learning from scientific text: Testing the generative drawing effect and the prognostic drawing effect. *Contemporary Educational Psychology, 39*(4), 275-286.

83. Allen, J., Gregory, A., Mikami, A., Lun, J., Hamre, B., & Pianta, R. (2013). Observations of effective teacher-student interactions in secondary school classrooms: Predicting student achievement with the classroom assessment scoring system-secondary. *School Psychology Review, 42*(1), 76-98.

84. Perry, J., Lundie, D., & Golder, G. (2019). Metacognition in schools: What does the literature suggest about the effectiveness of teaching metacognition in schools? *Educational Review, 71*(4), 483-500.

85. Topor, D. R., Keane, S. P., Shelton, T. L., & Calkins, S. D. (2010). Parent involvement and student academic performance: A multiple mediational analysis. *Journal of Prevention & Intervention in the Community, 38*(3), 183-197.

86. Hsee, C. K., & Hastie, R. (2006). Decision and experience: Why don't we choose what makes us happy? *Trends in Cognitive Sciences, 10*(1), 31-37.

87. Parker, P. D., Marsh, H. W., Thoemmes, F., & Biddle, N. (2019). The negative year in school effect: Extending scope and strengthening causal claims. *Journal of Educational Psychology, 111*(1), 118-130.

88. Yan, V. X., Thai, K. P., & Bjork, R. A. (2014). Habits and beliefs that guide self-regulated learning: Do they vary with mindset? *Journal of Applied Research in Memory and Cognition, 3*(3), 140-152.

89. Chandler, P., & Sweller, J. (1992). The split-attention effect as a factor in the design of instruction. *British Journal of Educational Psychology, 62*(2), 233-246.

90. Stiglic, N., & Viner, R. M. (2019). Effects of screentime on the health and well-being of children and adolescents: A systematic review of reviews. *BMJ Open, 9*(1), 1-15.

91. Butler, A. C. (2018). Multiple-choice testing in education: Are the best practices for assessment also good for learning? *Journal of Applied Research in Memory and Cognition, 7*(3), 323-331.

92. Short, M. A., Gradisar, M., Lack, L. C., Wright, H. R., & Chatburn, A. (2013). Estimating adolescent sleep patterns: Parent reports versus adolescent self-report surveys, sleep diaries, and actigraphy. *Nature and Science of Sleep, 5*, 23-26.

93. Fisher, A. V., Godwin, K. E., & Seltman, H. (2014). Visual environment, attention allocation, and learning in young children: When too much of a good thing may be bad. *Psychological Science, 25*(7), 1362-1370.

94. Cooper, H., Nye, B., Charlton, K., Lindsay, J., & Greathouse, S. (1996). The effects of summer vacation on achievement test scores: A narrative and meta-analytic review. *Review of Educational Research, 66*(3), 227-268.

95. Katzir, M., Emanuel, A., & Liberman, N. (2020). Cognitive performance is enhanced if one knows when the task will end. *Cognition, 197*, 104189.

96. Rohrer, D. (2012). Interleaving helps students distinguish among similar concepts. *Educational Psychology Review, 24*(3), 355-367.

97. Skipper, Y., & Douglas, K. (2015). The influence of teacher feedback on children's perceptions of student-teacher relationships. *British Journal of Educational Psychology, 85*(3), 276-288.

98. Study 98: Kahneman, D., Fredrickson, B. L., Schreiber, C. A., & Redelmeier, D. A. (1993). When more pain is preferred to less: Adding a better end. *Psychological Science, 4*(6), 401-405.

99. Wang, Y., Jones, B. F., & Wang, D. (2019). Early-career setback and future career impact. *Nature Communications, 10*(1), 1-10.

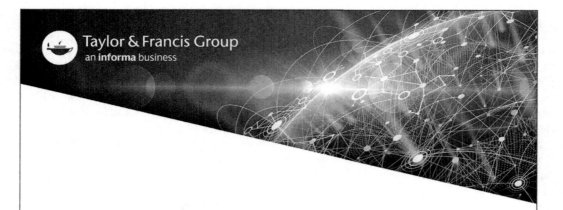

31503700906453

UK Mail

Royal mail

Printed in Great Britain
by Amazon